W9-AAW-520

BATTLE OF BRITAIN

BATTLE OF BRITAIN

CHARLES MESSENGER

DORSET PRESS

Page 1: *Heinkels head for their target.*

Previous page: Hurricanes of 85 Squadron RAF.

Below: *Ground crew making a Hurricane ready for battle.*

This editon published by
Dorset Press,
A division of Marboro Books Corp.

Produced by
Brompton Books Corporation
15 Sherwood Place
Greenwich CT 06830

ISBN 0-86124-625-X

Printed in Hong Kong

CONTENTS

— INTRODUCTION —

This year marks the 50th anniversary of a short period in British history in which Winston Churchill said at its outset: 'Let us therefore brace ourselves to our duties, and so bear ourselves that, if the British Empire and its Commonwealth last for a thousand years, men will still say: "This was their finest hour."'

Only the most senior generation now remember what the atmosphere was like during those summer and autumn days of 1940 when Britain and the far flung Dominions and colonies stood alone against the Axis. The Germans, in particular, had tasted nothing but the heady wine of victory in nine months of war, while British successes had been small and few and far between. There seemed to be little that could stop Hitler from crossing the English Channel and achieving his final objective in the west, the subjugation of Britain. Yet, in spite of the German efforts, it did not happen.

Much of the credit for this must be given to the Prime Minister himself, for his own dogged determination and obstinacy with which he imbued the British people through a series of inspired speeches. Tribute, too, must be paid to the people themselves who refused to be cowed either by threats or the munitions rained down upon them from the air. The uniformed services, too, also played their part, but none more so than RAF Fighter Command, especially the Spitfire and Hurricane pilots of many nationalities who climbed into the air day after day to keep the much vaunted Luftwaffe at bay.

The Battle of Britain has long been regarded as a David and Goliath contest of triumph in adversity, which in many ways it was. It was also a battle fought at high speed, which required not just the quickest of human reaction but also the application of what were then some of the frontiers of science. Above all it is a classic example of total war, where the many could only stand by and bear most of the punishment while the few fought it out.

In Britain today, the battle is still remembered and has its special day in the year, 15 September. The Royal Air Force church of St Clement Danes in London's Strand has a special Battle of Britain Memorial Window to commemorate the Few. Outside it is a statue of Air Chief Marshal Baron Dowding of Bentley Priory GCB GCVO CMG, widely recognised as the architect of the British victory, which was unveiled only in 1987. The Royal Air Force Museum has its own special Battle of Britain Display, and those who attend air displays will be familiar with the RAF's Battle of Britain Flight of Spitfire, Hurricane and Lancaster. Many RAF stations still have a Spitfire or Hurricane as their gate guardian. Finally, there are the veterans of the battle, the Battle of Britain Fighter Association, who continue to thrive and who also hold reunions with those they fought against, the members of *Luftflotten 2, 3,* and 5. That they do this is in part to recognise that courage was not merely the province of one side alone.

This book is an attempt to describe the Battle of Britain in its various phases. Although it is primarily concerned with the air battles that were fought by day in the skies over southern England, it recognises that the battle closely involved many other than air-crew, and in all walks of life. If the book has a message, it is that in its basest of activities, war, that humankind often displays its very highest qualities.

Above: *Spitfire Is, recognisable by the two bladed propellor. They entered RAF service in 1938.*

Left: *Tower Bridge, London, with burning Docklands behind, September 1940.*

Right: *Heavy Ack Ack in action against the Luftwaffe. By mid-August 1940 over 1200 of these guns were deployed to defend British skies.*

WITH A FIGHTER SQUADRON

by Wing Commander Douglas Bader

The following is an extract from a broadcast given by the late Wing Commander Sir Douglas Bader shortly before he was shot down and captured by the Germans in 1941.

I'd like to tell you something about the boys in my squadron. They're grand lads, every one of them. About 75 per cent, are Canadians and many of them came over to this country a year or two before the war to join the R.A.F. Several worked their way across, at least two of them on cattle-boats, and they all came here to do what they'd wanted to do since they were youngsters – to fly.

Since the war started they've shown that they can fight as well as they fly, and between them they've already won six of the nine D.F.C.s which have been awarded to the squadron. One holder of the D.F.C. is from Victoria, British Columbia. Another, who has won a bar to his D.F.C., comes from Calgary, Alberta. Others come from Toronto, Vancouver and Saskatoon. There's never been a happier or more determined crowd of fighter pilots, and, as an Englishman, I'm very proud to have the honour of leading them.

I shan't soon forget the first time the squadron was in action under my leadership. It was on August 30th, and I detailed the plot from Calgary to take his section of three Hurricanes up to keep thirty Me. 110's busy. "O.K., O.K.," he said with obvious relish, and away he streaked to deal with that vastly superior number of enemy fighters. When I saw him afterwards, his most vivid impression was of one German aircraft which he had sent crashing into a greenhouse.

Soon we spotted one large formation, and it was rather an awe-inspiring sight – particularly to anyone who hadn't previously been in action. We didn't adopt any set rule in attacking them – we just worked on the axiom that the shortest distance between two points is a straight line. I led the attack and went for what I think was the third block of six from the back. And *did* those Huns break up! In a few seconds there was utter confusion. They broke up all over the sky. As I went through, the section I aimed at fanned out. I can't give you an exact sequence of events, but I know that the Canadian pilot who followed immediately behind took the one that broke away to the left, while I took the one that broke away to the right. The third man in our line went straight through and gave the rear gunner of a Hun in one of the middle blocks an awful shock. Then the other boys followed on and things really began to get moving.

Now there's one curious thing about this air fighting. One minute you see hundreds of aeroplanes in the sky, and the next minute there's nothing. All you can do is to look through your sights at your particular target – and look in your mirror too, if you are sensible, for any Messerschmitts which might be trying to get on to your tail. Well, that particular battle lasted about five or ten minutes, and then, quite suddenly, the sky was clear of aircraft.

When we got down we totted up the score. We had destroyed twelve enemy aircraft with our nine Hurricanes. And when we examined our aircraft there wasn't a single bullet hole in any of them.

Above left: *The legendary legless ace Douglas Bader, who led the largely Canadian 242 Squadron during the Battle.*

Above: *Hurricane pilots of 1(RCAF) Squadron. Not only were the pilots Canadian, but the aircraft were built in Canada.*

Right: *Squadron Leader E A McNab, CO of 1 (RCAF) Squadron, on 12 September 1940. His squadron would play a leading part in the battles of 15 September.*

CHAPTER I
THE STAGE IS SET

Cutting their teeth – No 1 Squadron RAF in France during winter 1939-40. Note that some of their Hurricanes have been fitted with the superior 3-blade airscrews.

LK L

Left: *Dunkirk after the evacuation. Note the abandoned British transport.*

Right: *Signs of defeat – an abandoned French Char B heavy tank.*

Below: *German motor-cycle troops during the overrunning of France, June 1940.*

June 3, 1940 marked the last day of Operation DYNAMO, the evacuation of the British Expeditionary Force (BEF) and Allied troops from Dunkirk. In all, some 220,000 British and 120,000 French and Belgian troops were transported across the English Channel to Britain during a period of eight days, but at a cost. The BEF had been forced to leave all its weapons, other than small arms, behind. Some 200 ships of all types had been lost and the RAF, in its efforts to keep the Luftwaffe off those waiting on the beaches, had had 177 aircraft shot down. Next day Prime Minister Winston Churchill made the first of his epic wartime speeches. 'We shall defend our island, whatever the cost may be, we shall fight on the beaches, we shall fight on the landing grounds, we shall fight in the fields and in the streets, we shall fight in the hills; we shall never surrender.'

In France, meanwhile, German eyes now looked south as the second phase of the campaign in the West, the defeat of France, opened. It was to be even briefer than the first, which had taken just over three weeks. German troops entered Paris, which had been declared an open city, on 14 June and two days later the French decided to seek an armistice. On 20 June, Italy, which had finally entered the war ten days before, invaded the French Riviera, and on the 22nd the French signed an armistice with Germany. Two days later they signed one with the Italians, and hostilities came to an end on 25 June. Britain, apart from her empire overseas and exiles from Occupied Europe, was alone.

Hitler hoped that the fall of France would bring Britain to her senses and that she would make peace, thus enabling him to concentrate on the overthrow of Russian Bolshevism. Indeed, the possibility that he might have to invade Britain never seems to have occurred to him during the preparations for the campaign in the West. His only utterance on how Britain should be treated if the land campaign in the West was successful had been in his Directive No 9 dated 29 November 1939. This laid down that the most

effective way of bringing about her defeat was by crippling her economy. This was to be achieved by naval and air attacks on ports, shipping, oil and food depots, and munitions factories. A supplement to this, issued by the German Armed Forces Chief of Staff, Wilhelm Keitel, on 26 May 1940 ordered attacks on British food supplies, the disruption of public services and destruction of the aircraft industry, but invasion was not mentioned. Churchill, however, made it clear that Britain was going to fight on. Accordingly, on 1 July 1940, Hitler issued a further directive. Invasion was possible 'providing that air superiority can be attained and certain other necessary conditions fulfilled'. He gave no date, but ordered preparations for invasion to begin immediately. He emphasised that as yet it was only a plan.

Much of the planning devolved on the shoulders of Army Chief of Staff Franz Halder, who likened the operation to a 'large-scale river crossing'. By 11 July he had produced a draft plan, which was approved by the Army Commander-in-Chief, Walter von Brauchitsch. On the basis of Halder's plan Hitler produced Directive No 16 on Operation SEALION on 16 July. It called for twenty divisions to land in Lyme Bay, west of Weymouth, on the coast between Portsmouth and Brighton and on that between Hastings and Dover. It was a very wide front and brought about strong objections from the German Navy's CinC, Erich Raeder, who argued that it would be impossible for his ships to give the necessary protection to the force. The directive made it clear, however, that an essential prerequisite was that the 'English Air Force must be so reduced morally and physically that it is unable to deliver any significant attack against the German crossing'. The Luftwaffe, though, had already opened its account.

On 5 June, as the German armies began to move south against the French, the Luftwaffe sent some fifty Heinkel (He) 111 bombers across the Channel to attack airfields and other military installations. Other such operations were mounted during the

month, but little damage was caused and the object appears to have been to perfect navigation systems, of which more later. On the 30th, Hermann Goering, as CinC of the Luftwaffe, issued *General Directive for the Operation of the Luftwaffe against England*. This reflected Hitler's Directive No 9 of November 1939. It recognised that Britain's economy would be best destroyed by cutting off her overseas trade. For this to be successful the Royal Air Force had to be destroyed. Time, however, was needed to regroup the Luftwaffe for a sustained campaign and in the meantime it would confine itself to nuisance operations and to attacking shipping in the English Channel so as to draw the RAF fighters up into battle. These began immediately and on 10 July there was a mid-Channel air battle involving over 100 aircraft. This day marks the official opening day of the Battle of Britain.

The Luftwaffe was to employ three *Luftflotten* (air fleets) during the battle. The main burden would be borne by Albert Kesselring's *Luftflotte 2*, based in the Low Countries and northern France, and Hugo Sperrle's *Luftflotte 3*, operating from bases in north-western France. Hans Jürgen Stumpff's *Luftflotte 5*, which was based in Norway and Denmark, would also be called upon. Exact figures on the numerical strength available vary, but a reasonably accurate breakdown by aircraft types is:

Bombers 1200
Dive-bombers 280
Single-engine fighters 760
Twin-engine fighters 220
Reconnaissance 130

This gives a total of 2600 aircraft, of which some 80 per cent would be serviceable at any one time. The *Luftflotten* themselves compromised a number of *Fleigerkorps*, and each of these commanded a

Left: *RAF Fairey Battles, which suffered grievously in France, attacking a German transport column.*

Right: *Field Marshal Erhard Milch (in uniform), Inspector General of the Luftwaffe and its prime organiser.*

Below: *France May 1940 – German infantry advancing on the Dunkirk perimeter.*

varying number of *Geschwaderen* (groups). A *Geschwader* had some seventy aircraft and was designated by type:

Kampfgeschwader (KG) – Bomber
Stukageschwader (StG) – Divebomber
Jagdgeschwader (JG) – Fighter
Zerstörergeschwader (ZG) – Destroyer

Three or four *Gruppen* made up a *Geschwader* and in each *Gruppe* there were three or four *Staffeln* (squadrons). The *Staffel* was the lowest element in the chain of command and usually had twelve aircraft.

The Luftwaffe itself in July 1940 was riding on the crest of the wave. Although it had only officially existed for less than ten years it was finely honed. At its head was the corpulent Hermann Goering. Yet, in World War I he had been a fighter ace and had commanded the famous von Richthofen Circus after the death in combat of its namesake, Germany's top scoring ace of the war. His position in the Nazi heirarchy and the fact that, unlike the other two armed services, the Luftwaffe was a National Socialist creation, gave it special status in Hitler's eyes. True, Goering's boast before Dunkirk that his aircraft could destroy the BEF on their own had proved an empty one, but the Luftwaffe's overall performance in Poland and the West was one to be proud of. Of the three *Luftflotte* commanders, only Sperrle had flown during the Great War, the other two having been soldiers who had transferred to the Luftwaffe on its formation in 1933. Nevertheless, Kesselring and Sperrle had successfully commanded their *Luftflotten* during the recent campaign in the West and Stumpff's *Luftflotte* had taken part in the invasion of Denmark and Norway.

As for the German aircrews, they were now highly experienced. Not only had many taken part in at least two of the three cam-

Above left: *General Wolfram Freiherr von Richthofen, nephew of the Red Baron and commander of* Fleigerkorps VIII.

Above: *Field Marshal Hugo Sperrle.*

Left: *General Ernst Udet, World War I ace and in charge of Luftwaffe equipment procurement.*

paigns in which Germany had been engaged since the outbreak of war, but some had had earlier combat experience as members of the *Kondor Legion* in Spain. Some, like Adolf Galland and Werner Mölders, were already aces with several 'kills' to their credit. Having so far swept everything before them they were confident in their ability quickly to break the back of the RAF. In order to foster their morale, a special song was written for those about to take part in the coming battle, *Wir fliegen gegen England* ('We fly against England').

Crucial to success was obviously the quality of the Luftwaffe's aircraft. The thinking behind Germany's air force was as a lever against her neighbours. Its very being was to be a threat sufficient for the countries bordering Germany to give way to Hitler's territorial and other demands. The need for quantity to present an effective deterrent and the view that war only against neighbouring countries was possible meant that the Luftwaffe was essentially a tactical rather than a strategic air force. The bombers with which the Luftwaffe was equipped, the Heinkel 111, Junkers 88 and Dornier 17 could hardly be called long range bombers, being able to fly some 800 miles with a 4000lb bombload. When compared to the British heavy bombers, the Stirling, Manchester and Halifax, then in the final stages of development and which had an average range of 1000 miles carrying 13,000lbs of bombs, the limitations of the German bombers become clear.

There was one other bomber which the Germans would use, the Junkers 87 Stuka divebomber. The concept of vertical bombing had originally been investigated by the Americans as a means of knocking out ships. The Stuka itself was the brainchild of Ernst Udet, the Luftwaffe's Chief of Supply and Procurement, who was inspired by a display by the Curtiss Hawk in America. The Stuka first saw action in the Spanish Civil War and during the Polish and Western campaigns had developed into a highly effective form of aerial artillery, although it was its effect on morale rather than the accuracy of its bombing which made its reputation.

The Luftwaffe had two fighters, both made by Messerschmitt, the Me109 and Me110. The latter was a 2-engine aircraft and termed a *Zerstörer* (destroyer). It was conceived primarily as a bomber escort and the emphasis was on range and armament. It had performed well in Poland and France, but, as would be demonstrated during the weeks to come, it had limitations in manoeuvrability. The Me109 was a horse of a different colour. When it first flew in 1935, it was more advanced in design than any other fighter flying at the time. Its combat superiority was demonstrated during the Spanish Civil War. In 1939 it broke the world air speed record, achieving 469mph, although this was a special version of the aircraft and the service types flew some 100mph slower. By 1940 the Luftwaffe was equipped with the Me109E Emil version, which was armed with 20mm cannon, rather than 7.92mm

Above: *Leading ace Werner Mölders (second left) after a successful sortie.*

Below: *Preparing for battle – Do17s somewhere in northern France.*

Above: *Vickers test pilot Jeffrey Quill, who would later distinguish himself in the Battle, at the controls of a Spitfire I.*

Left: *The first prototype Spitfire. Its designer, Reginald Mitchell, died of cancer before the aircraft went into production.*

machine guns. Highly manoeuvrable, with a fast rate of climb and dive, it was a formidable aircraft. With these seemingly well proven aircraft at their disposal it is no wonder that the Luftwaffe faced the coming battle with the utmost confidence.

As German servicemen stood at Cap Gris Nez, where the English Channel is at its narrowest, and gazed across the water at the white cliffs of Dover shimmering in the summer heat, they wondered what their enemy was up to and why he would not give up the fight. Curiously, perhaps, there was almost a sense of relief in Britain now she was alone. Shorn of the problems of coalition warfare the path ahead seemed clearer than it had been before the fall of France. The British were now bracing themselves for the expected cross-Channel invasion. Defences were being hastily constructed around the coasts; literally thousands of small concrete strongpoints, known as pillboxes, many of which still survive today, were springing up all over the country; all signposts had been removed from road junctions, and larger fields of pasture strewn with old cars and other obstacles to impede enemy aircraft or gliders trying to land. The Army was desperately trying to make good its equipment losses in France and had now been joined by the Local Defence Volunteers, shortly to be retitled the Home Guard, but better known today as Dad's Army, a part-time force equipped with a motley selection of weapons. The Royal Navy, while not prepared to risk its capital ships, which remained at the Home Fleet wartime anchorage at Scapa Flow in the Orkney Islands, to air attack and mines, was organising cruisers and destroyers based at Sheerness, Harwich and Portsmouth to attack the invasion fleet when it sailed. What all realised, just as the Germans did, was that for SEALION to succeed the Germans had to achieve air superiority. The only weapon in the British armoury which could prevent this was RAF Fighter Command.

The man who would bear the main responsibility for waging the fight was the Air Officer-in-Chief of Fighter Command, Air Chief Marshal Sir Hugh Dowding. Aged 58 in 1940, he had been in charge of Fighter Command since its creation in July 1936. When his command was formed British air policy was still based on the

premise that, to use Prime Minister Stanley Baldwin's famous comment in the House of Commons in November 1932, 'the bomber will always get through'. Hence, the RAF's prewar expansion plans gave priority to the bomber over the fighter. Dowding's previous job had been responsibility for research and supply and he came to Bentley Priory, the country house at Stanmore on the north-west outskirts of London which housed his headquarters, aware of two technical developments which had the potential of drastically reducing the seeming invincibility of the bomber.

The problem with the fighter up until the mid 1930s was that it still retained the wooden structure and biplane design of 1914-18. This meant that it had a relatively slow rate of climb. Added to this were that the only means of gaining warning of an impending bomber attack were visual and oral. This meant that even if a force of bombers was spotted they were inevitably too close to their target for the fighters to be scrambled to intercept them before they attacked. The only way to get over this problem was through aerial standing patrols of fighters, a prohibitively expensive use of resources, especially since there was no guarantee that they could intercept.

The Schneider Trophy speed competition for seaplanes had been won by the monoplane Supermarine S-6b three times in a row during 1927-1931 and it was out of this success that the Super-

Above: *A prototype Hurricane. Designed by Sidney Camm, it entered RAF service in early 1938*

Right: *Blenheim MKIs of 604 Squadron RAuxAF, which was based at Middle Wallop, Hampshire for much of the Battle.*

Above: *'Scramble!'*

Right: *Preparing for take off. A Spitfire I is manoeuvred into position.*

Left: *Air Chief Marshal Sir Hugh Dowding, AOCinC Fighter Command, who masterminded the Battle.*

marine Spitfire and Hawker Hurricane evolved. Dowding knew that their all-metal construction and eight machine guns could radically alter the balance, as the Germans were already displaying the Me109. It was merely a question of time, whether there would be enough before war came to complete their development and manufacture sufficient numbers.

The second technical development dealt with the other half of the problem, that of timely warning. It was a Scottish scientist, Robert Watson Watt, who headed a team at the Radio Research Station, part of the National Physical Laboratory, who evolved a solution. In February 1935, as a result of a number of virtually unrelated occurrences, he produced a paper, *Detection and Location of Aircraft by Radio Method* in which he proposed that pulsed radio signals from a powerful transmitter could be reflected from an aircraft at a range of up to 100 miles and detected by using a radio receiver. Not only would the aircraft's presence be detected, but its range, bearing and height obtained as well. So impressed was the Air Ministry that, after a simple demonstration, it provided money for the further development of the system. By spring 1936 the system, called radiolocation or radio direction finding (RDF) in those days but changed, through agreement with the Americans later in the war, to radar, had been made workable. Now began the task of constructing, under the utmost secrecy, a chain of RDF stations along the south and east coasts of England under the title of the Chain Home network. Dowding was well aware of Chain Home when he arrived at Bentley Priory and this made him even

more determined to obtain an increase in the proportion of fighter aircraft to be included in the RAF's ever changing expansion schemes as war approached.

By the end of 1938 Dowding had managed to win his case insofar that government approval was given for 50 fighter squadrons by March 1942, and he was promised 40 of these by March 1939. This compared with 85 bomber squadrons, of which 57 would be formed by March 1939 and reflected initial priority being given to fighters. His stand had, however, made him a number of enemies and he was getting on in years. In July 1938 he was told that he would be retired at the end of June 1939, but the following February, in view of the worsening international situation, this was deferred. He remained in command once the war began, but was then told that he would definitely be retired in mid-July 1940. On 5 July 1940, however, Dowding received a letter from Sir Cyril Newall, Chief of the Air Staff, asking him to remain at his post until October.

The state of his command at the end of Dunkirk had given Dowding much cause for concern. It was inevitable that more of his squadrons should have been drawn into the battle for France than he would have wanted. He had had to surrender ten squadrons, including two Hurricane, at the outbreak of war to the Advanced Air Striking Force which accompanied the BEF to France. Once the 'balloon went up' on 10 May further fighter squadrons were sent across the Channel and then there had been Dunkirk. Indeed, by the end of the campaign he had lost 453 Hurricanes and Spitfires alone, but what was to be more critical, had a shortfall of 362 pilots.

Shortly after he became prime minister in May 1940, Churchill created a new ministry, the Ministry of Aircraft Production, and placed his old friend the newspaper magnate Lord Beaverbrook in

Above: *Trafford Leigh-Mallory, the outspoken and controversial AOC No 12 Group. Photograph taken in 1944 when he was Eisenhower's air commander for the Normandy landings.*

Right: *The eyes of Britain's defences – a Chain Home radar station, the aerials on the left were transmitters; those on the right receivers. They proved remarkably difficult to put out of action.*

Right: *ARP wardens inspect children's gasmasks. The prewar belief that the Luftwaffe would drop gas bombs took time to die.*

Below right: *Inside a Chain Home station.*

charge. One of the myths of the Battle of Britain is that Beaverbrook dramatically transformed the industry within a matter of weeks. In fact, although production had lagged behind monthly targets for the first few months of the war, in April 1940, before Churchill came to power, fighter production exceeded its monthly target and maintained this through the course of the Battle of Britain. True, the difference between the two rates did increase under Beaverbrook's dynamic leadership, helped, perhaps, by the fact that his son, Max Aitken, would take a leading part in the battle as a fighter squadron commander. But the real change came from the fruition of prewar expediency plans, which had created a system of 'shadow factories', and these had taken time to convert from the production of other, peacetime goods to aircraft components.

Pilots, however, could not merely be factory produced. Not everyone has the particular in-built qualities to be able to fly an aircraft, let alone have the necessary attributes to be a fighter pilot. To produce a fully trained fighter pilot took about a year, and only a small proportion of those accepted for initial flying training graduated at the end. The training organisation had not expanded at sufficient pace to cope with the sharp rise in aircrew losses during the French campaign and there was a worrying shortfall. It was pilot rather than aircraft losses which would concern Dowding more during the coming battle.

Nevertheless, the pause in June after an intensive May enabled Fighter Command to gather breath and rebuild its strength to an extent. Dowding had calculated that he needed a minimum of 53 squadrons to defend Britain effectively, but had been reduced to 37 by the end of May. In the space of a month, however, he had managed to increase this to 52 squadrons (19 Spitfire, 25 Hurricane, two Defiant and six Blenheim). This gave a total of 644 serviceable aircraft.

At the beginning of July RAF Fighter Command was organised into three groups, with a fourth, No 10, which had been forming since January, becoming operational at the end of July. Covering south-east England and very much in the front line was No 11 Group. This was commanded by Air Vice Marshal Keith Park, a New Zealander who had distinguished himself as a fighter pilot during World War 1. He was well known to Dowding, having been his chief of staff until spring 1940. To his north, and covering eastern England was Trafford Leigh-Mallory's No 12 Group. Leigh-Mallory had assumed command in 1937, although up until then his speciality had been army co-operation. He had a reputation for outspokenness and did not get on with Park. North yet again, and responsible for Scotland and northern England was Richard Saul's No 13 Group. He himself had been a Royal Naval Air Service pilot in World War 1. Finally, to cover the south-west and Wales was Sir Quintin Brand's No 10 Group. Brand was a South African who had been knighted in 1920 after making the first flight from London to Cape Town. He had also shot down a German bomber during the last raid on London in 1918.

Each group commanded a number of stations at which were normally based two or three squadrons. The squadron itself usually had 12 aircraft, divided into two flights each of two three-aircraft sections, and four, later eight, reserve aircraft.

Yet, RAF Fighter Command's organisation for battle consisted of much more than just the squadrons. Firstly, there were the 'eyes' of the Command, which gave the necessary early warning of an impending raid. By July 1940 Chain Home consisted of thirty radar stations, which were controlled by No 60 Group. They passed information directly to HQ Fighter Command's operations room at Bentley Priory. There were two types of station. The first, which made up the CH chain, gave long range coverage, while the other, the CHL chain, which operated on a much shorter wavelength, concentrated primarily on low flying aircraft, which the CH chain was unable to detect. Backing up the radar were the observation posts of the Royal Observer Corps. These were littered throughout the country and passed details of sightings of enemy aircraft to their local Group operations room, who then sent this to Bentley Priory.

Two further intelligence agencies existed. Firstly, there was Bletchley Park, home of the Government Code and Cipher School. This devoted its attention to deciphering the codes used by the Germans with their Enigma cipher machines. Some writers have claimed that Ultra, as this work was codenamed, played a decisive part in the Battle of Britain. It is true that the Luftwaffe was careless with the use of its versions of the Enigma cipher, and some valuable intelligence was gained from the decrypts. On the other hand, because the Luftwaffe formations taking part in the battle were relatively static, most information and orders were sent by landline and could not, of course, be monitored. More significant, though, was the work of what became known as the RAF Y Service. This was made up of German speaking radio operators who monitored the Luftwaffe's aircraft frequencies. They could advise Groups on the height of approaching aircraft and work out which formation they were from. Through this their return route could often be deduced and fighters positioned to intercept them.

From the fighter pilot's point of view it was the sector control room which was the most important. Each group had a number of these, and kept them briefed on details of raids as they built up. The sector controller then scrambled the squadrons and directed their aircraft to the best position from which to make their attacks.

Opposite top: *Preparing a Spitfire for the next sortie.*

Opposite bottom: *A Fighter Command control room.*

Above: *Refuelling a Ju87 Stuka.*

Left: *Royal Observer Corps post.*

Right: *'Smiling Albert' Kesselring of* Luftflotte 2.

Two other elements must also be mentioned. Firstly, there was RAF Balloon Command, which was placed under Fighter Command's control for the battle. By summer 1940 the barrage balloon skyline was familiar to many Britons, especially if they lived in and around large towns and cities. Their object was to prevent enemy aircraft from making low flying and hence more accurate attacks. Clearly it was vital that their activities were closely integrated in order to prevent RAF aircraft from being taken unawares and flying into the steel cables which tethered the balloons. There was also General 'Tim' Pile's Anti-Aircraft Command. This consisted of some 1200 heavy anti-aircraft guns, organised into seven AA divisions, and with batteries deployed throughout the United Kingdom and Northern Ireland. Pile's headquarters was colocated with Dowding's at Stanmore and in every operations room, at whatever level, there was an AA Command representative present to ensure that AA guns did not engage friendly aircraft.

With such a large organisation, involving so many agencies, good communications were vital. The fact that they worked as well

Above: *Keith Park, whose No 11 Group bore the brunt of the Battle.*

as they did – teleprinter, landline, radio – was a tribute to the communications experts who planned and laid out the system. They are unsung heroes of the Battle.

The final two factors in the equation were the aircraft and their pilots. On 2 May 1940 the British had been lucky enough to capture an Me109E intact. It was immediately taken to the Royal Aircraft Establishment at Farnborough for evaluation. Tests confirmed the suspicion that it was superior to the Hurricane, except in turning circle, and manoeuvrability at low altitude. With the Spitfire it was much more marginal. The Me109E had a faster rate of climb up to 20,000ft, after which the Spitfire was superior, and was also faster in the dive. On the other hand, the Spitfire was much more manoeuvrable and had a tighter turning circle. The Me109E's cannon also packed more punch than the eight 0.303in machine guns with which the Spitfire and Hurricane were armed. What these tests did reveal was the necessity to change the existing two-bladed fixed-pitch wooden airscrew with which the British fighters were fitted for a metal three-bladed variable pitch propellor. This gave improved climb and speed and almost all RAF fighters had converted to it by the beginning of July. The other two types of aircraft in Fighter Command service, the Blenheim in its fighter version and the Defiant, were of little consequence, but later performed usefully as night fighters.

The pilots were a mixture of prewar regular RAF and the 'weekend fliers' of the Royal Air Force Volunteer Reserve (RAFVR), with an increasing number who had joined at the outbreak of war. The battles over France had given a number, especially Hurricane pilots, much combat experience in a very short time, but some squadrons had lost heavily and needed the lull in order to rest and refurbish. Dowding was conscious of the need to spread the experience around his squadrons and there was a high degree of inter-posting between squadrons during June to ensure that this happened. Those who had already seen action had that added confidence which comes with experience. It had also increased their faith in their aircraft. All this quickly spread to those who had yet to face an enemy aircraft. Morale was, as with their opposite numbers across the Channel, high.

Now, as July opened, there were signs that the lull was coming to an end. Attacks against convoys in the Channel increased. On 3 July RAF Manston, one of the frontline airfields in Kent, was subjected to bombing attack, and coat trailing Me109s were increasingly spotted around the south coast of England.

Below: *Refuel and rearm – at work on a Hurricane.*

Verband	Auftrag
I/154	Portsmouth
II/154	
K.G.54	
K.G.54	

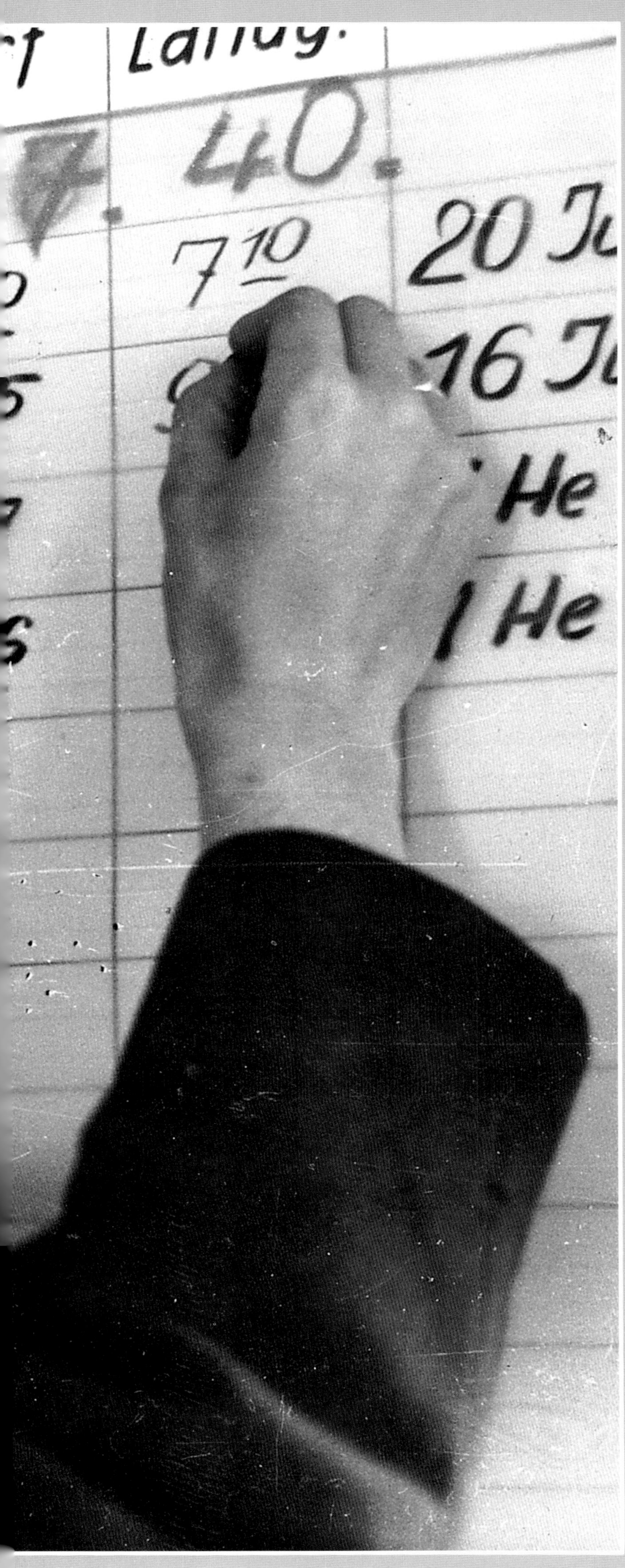

CHAPTER II

THE FIRST SHOTS

Day 4 and Kampfgeschwader 54*'s first targets are shipping.*

Wednesday 10 July 1940 dawned cloudy, with intermittent driving rain. It was not a day that promised much air activity. Even so, German reconnaissance aircraft, Do17s and Do215s, as well as Ju88s, were active from first light onwards, checking on the weather and photographing potential targets. One of them, a Do17, was successfully intercepted and shot down by a section of Spitfires from 66 Squadron based at Coltishall in Norfolk. Another Do17, this time off the Kent coast, spotted a convoy of merchant ships about to enter the Dover Straits and the English Channel. The crew radioed the details back to their base, but the Me109s escorting the Dornier now found themselves scrapping with a flight of Spitfires from 74 Squadron at Manston. Two Spitfires were damaged, but the Do17 was also hit.

The convoy triggered significant Luftwaffe reaction. Apart from helping to throttle Britain's maritime trade, the Germans hoped that attacks on Channel convoys would provoke the RAF into sending fighters to protect the ships. Close to their bases, and having drawn the British fighters away from theirs, the Luftwaffe fighters then stood a reasonable chance of driving their opponents into the sea. In this way the RAF fighter strength could be whittled down. On this day an Me109 *Staffel* was sent across the Channel early, while preparations for the attack on the convoy were got underway. They clashed with Spitfires, and all returned, having damaged one British fighter.

The main battle over the convoy took place in the early afternoon. Dornier Do17s, escorted by Me110s, had been sent to attack the convoy, while above them wheeled Me109s. Five RAF squadrons, Spitfire and Hurricane, were scrambled, and managed to get in among the Dorniers. As the battle drifted towards Dover, four Do17s and an Me109 were shot down at the cost of a Hurricane before the Germans turned for home. One ship in the convoy was sunk. The honours in this engagement lay with the RAF. During the action a BBC reporter happened to be in Dover making a broadcast. He interrupted it:

'There's one coming down in flames – there somebody's hit a German – and he's coming down – there's a long streak – he's coming down completely out of control – a long streak of smoke – ah, there's a man baled out by parachute – the pilot's baled out by parachute – he's a Junkers 87 and he's going slap into the sea and there he goes – sm-a-sh . . . Oh boy, I've never seen anything so good as this – the RAF fighters have really got these boys taped.' This was certainly heartening to those who heard it on their radios, but elsewhere the Germans enjoyed better success.

Hugo Sperrle ordered 63 bombers to attack South Wales ports. By sending his aircraft on a dog leg into the Atlantic and approaching from the west, Sperrle caught the British defences napping, caused heavy damage to the docks at Swansea and, on their return flight, the Cornish port of Falmouth. Not a single German bomber

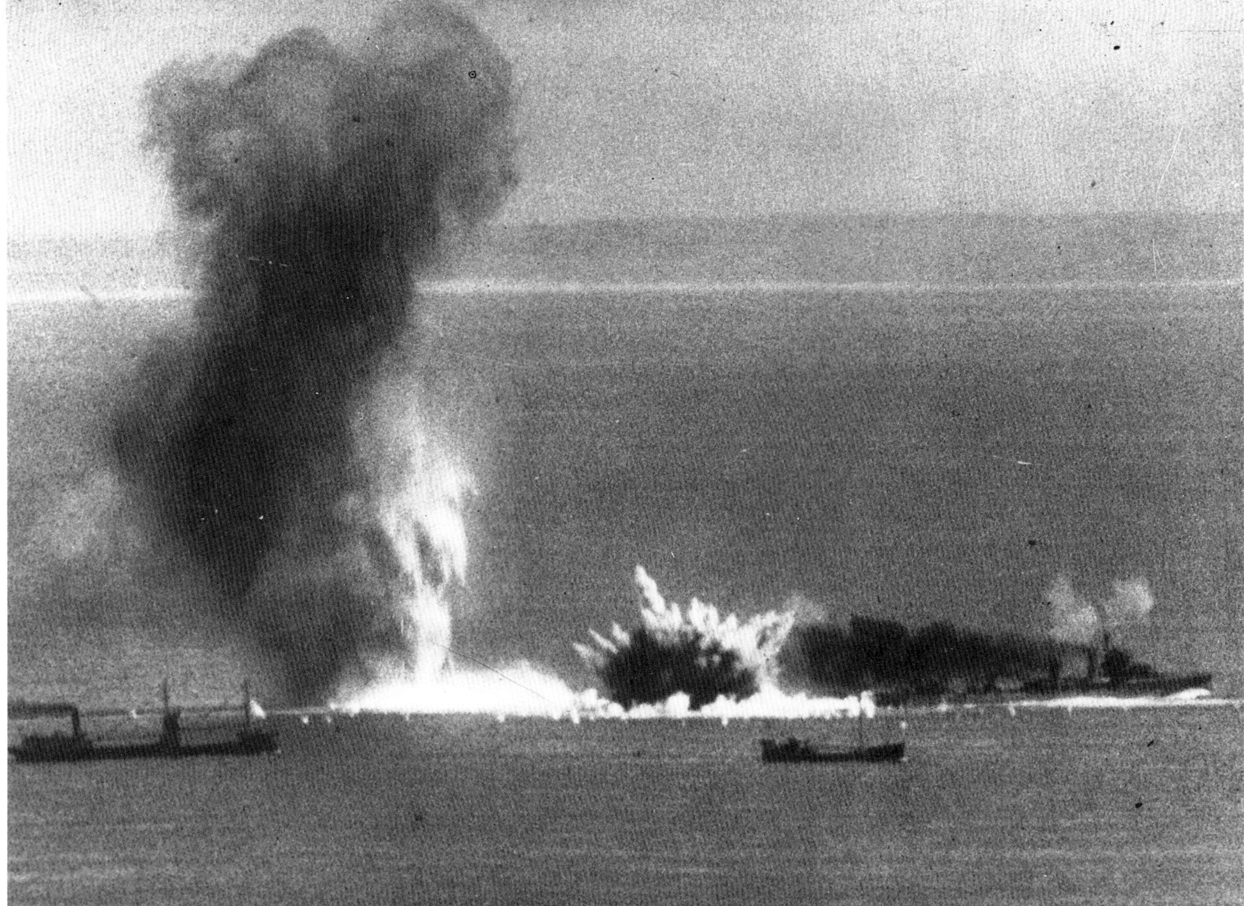

Above: *Portsmouth dockyard under attack. Note the bomb splashes.*

Top left: *An Me110 from II/ZG76 over the English coast. This* Gruppe *was part of Luftflotte 2.*

Left: *14 July 1940 and Channel convoy CW6 comes under attack. One destroyer was crippled, one merchant vessel sunk and two others damaged.*

was even damaged. There were other smaller clashes during the day and by the end of it 13 German aircraft had been lost, as against six British. Also on this first day, Beaverbrook issued a plea to the British people to surrender their aluminium pots and pans and other household goods so they could be turned into aircraft.

The next few days did not produce quite such frenetic activity. Widespread fog and cloud were one reason for this. Another was that Goering was not yet ready to commit his full force. Even so, there were clashes. A Stuka raid on the Dorset naval base at Portland saw two Ju87s and two Me110s shot down, but earlier in the day, during another Stuka attack, Me109s dealt roughly with a Spitfire flight, shooting two down. The following day German bombers attacked an east coast convoy and saw off Hurricanes sent up to intercept them. A few days later the Defiants made their first appearance in the battle.

The Boulton-Paul Defiant was an aircraft built round a hydraulically operated dorsal mounted turret armed with four 0.303 inch machine guns, the theory being that this would keep enemy aircraft off the aircraft's back. It had had some success in France, where 264 Squadron claimed 28 victims in one day. The Luftwaffe soon got wise to it, as was demonstrated by the experience of the other Defiant squadron, No 141, on 19 July. It had just been deployed to Hawkinge, outside Folkestone, and was ordered on Channel patrol. Two *Staffeln* of Me109s attacked nine Defiants and quickly sent six down into the sea, and badly damaged another, killing its gunner.

Top: *Boulton Paul Defiants of 264 Squadron. These proved easy meat for the Me109 and suffered accordingly.*

Above: *A British pilot downed in the Channel is taken aboard a German air-sea rescue boat.*

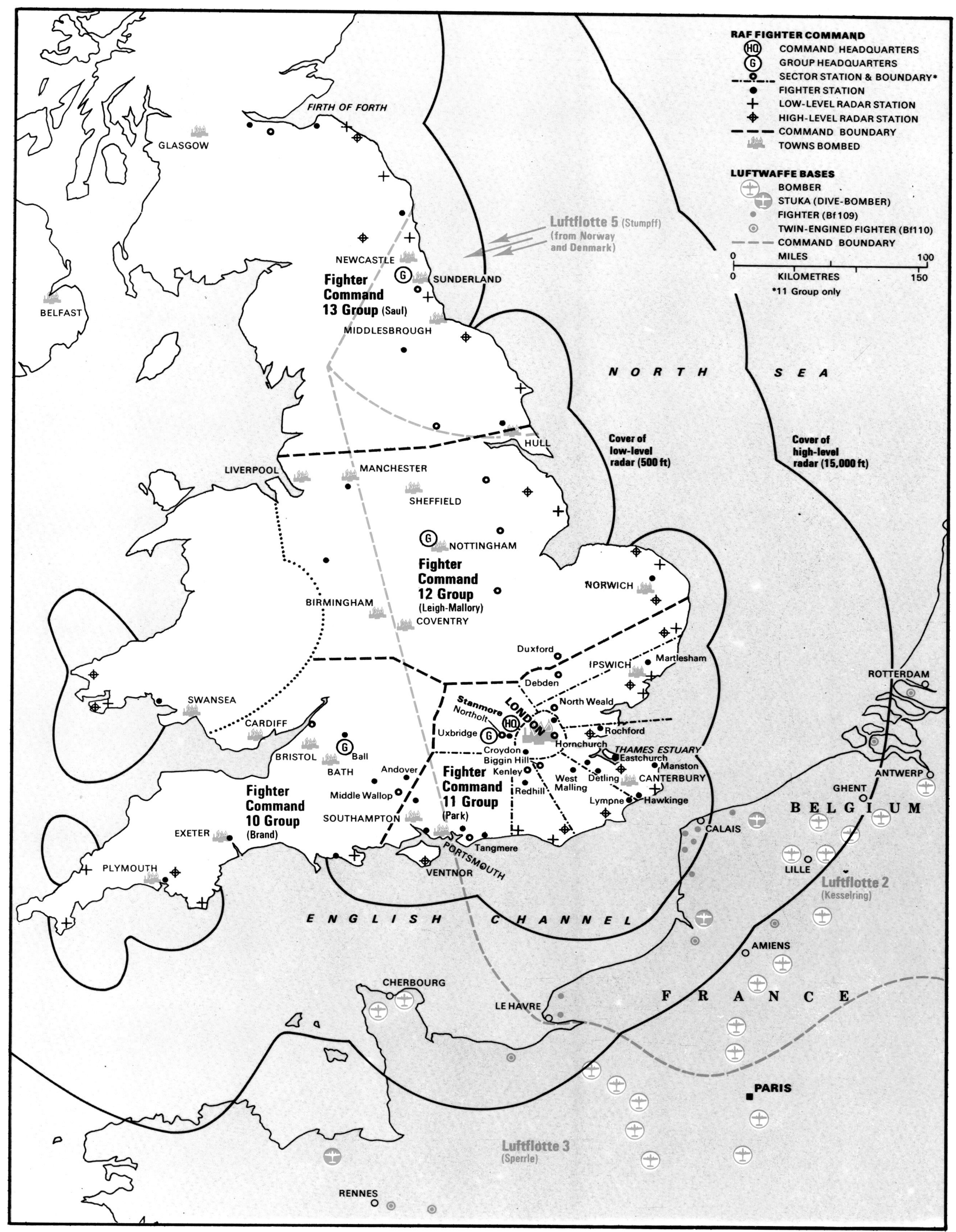
RAF FIGHTER COMMAND
COMMAND HEADQUARTERS
GROUP HEADQUARTERS
SECTOR STATION & BOUNDARY*
FIGHTER STATION
LOW-LEVEL RADAR STATION
HIGH-LEVEL RADAR STATION
COMMAND BOUNDARY
TOWNS BOMBED
LUFTWAFFE BASES
BOMBER
STUKA (DIVE-BOMBER)
FIGHTER (Bf109)
TWIN-ENGINED FIGHTER (Bf110)
COMMAND BOUNDARY
MILES
KILOMETRES
*11 Group only
FIRTH OF FORTH
GLASGOW
BELFAST
NEWCASTLE
SUNDERLAND
MIDDLESBROUGH
Fighter Command 13 Group (Saul)
Luftflotte 5 (Stumpff) (from Norway and Denmark)
NORTH SEA
Cover of low-level radar (500 ft)
Cover of high-level radar (15,000 ft)
HULL
LIVERPOOL
MANCHESTER
SHEFFIELD
NOTTINGHAM
Fighter Command 12 Group (Leigh-Mallory)
NORWICH
BIRMINGHAM
COVENTRY
Duxford
IPSWICH
Martlesham
Debden
North Weald
Stanmore
Northolt
LONDON
Rochford
Uxbridge
Hornchurch
THAMES ESTUARY
Eastchurch
Manston
CANTERBURY
Croydon
Biggin Hill
Kenley
West Malling
Detling
Redhill
Lympne
Hawkinge
Fighter Command 11 Group (Park)
SWANSEA
CARDIFF
BRISTOL
Ball
BATH
Andover
Middle Wallop
SOUTHAMPTON
Fighter Command 10 Group (Brand)
EXETER
PLYMOUTH
Tangmere
PORTSMOUTH
VENTNOR
ENGLISH CHANNEL
ROTTERDAM
ANTWERP
GHENT
BELGIUM
CALAIS
LILLE
Luftflotte 2 (Kesselring)
AMIENS
CHERBOURG
LE HAVRE
FRANCE
PARIS
Luftflotte 3 (Sperrle)
RENNES

Hitler, though, still hoped that the British might think again, even though he had by now issued his directive on SEALION. On the evening of the 19th, he made a speech in the Reichstag. Having poured scorn on Churchill, he went on to say: 'In this hour I feel it to be my duty before my own conscience to appeal once more to reason and common sense in Great Britain as much as anywhere. I consider myself in a position to make this appeal since I am not the vanquished begging favours, but the victor speaking in the name of reason. I can see no reason why this war must go on.' During the course of his speech he also announced the elevation of twelve of

Top left: *A symbolic shot of an Me110 over the White Cliffs of Dover.*

Left: *Me110s, undistracted by the shipping beneath them, race across the Channel towards the English coast.*

Above: *'Now thrive the armourers' – 500kg bombs being prepared for arming Ju87 Stukas.*

his generals to the rank of Field Marshal. These included Kesselring and Sperrle. The British response to his speech came virtually within the hour from the BBC German service. It was an emphatic dismissal; the British would fight on.

Next day Goering summoned his three *Luftflotte* commanders to Berlin to discuss their role in Hitler's Directive No 16. The only addition to the brief that they already had was attacks on British warships other than those escorting convoys.

The skirmishing over the Channel continued to rumble on. The convoys using it were beginning to suffer increasingly, especially

from the Stukas. On 20 July, after feinting against Dover, the Stukas struck convoy CW7 between Folkestone and Dover in the early evening. Among the escorts was the destroyer *Brazen*, which was fatally hit by a bomb exploding under her hull, but she managed to take three Stukas with her. A merchant vessel was also sunk and two others damaged. RAF fighters managed, however, to down four Me109s for the loss of two of their own. Five days later there were even more intensive attacks on convoy CW8. It was attacked by some 90 Stukas and Ju88s with fighter escort. Five ships were sunk and a further five damaged. Spitfires and Hurricanes, outnumbered by as much as four to one, managed to gain some revenge, but also lost some of their own. German E-boats then moved in to finish the damaged merchantmen. Two destroyers set sail from Dover and managed to see them off, in spite of coming under fire from German coastal batteries at Cap Gris Nez. Returning to Dover, they were themselves attacked by Stukas. Both were severely damaged and had to be towed in to harbour by tugs.

Dowding, of course, could have provided the convoys with more comprehensive air cover and have sent up more aircraft when they were attacked. He knew only too well, however, that the Luftwaffe was still biding its time and that the main assault on Britain was yet to come. He saw it as vital to risk no more of his fighters and their even more precious pilots than was absolutely necessary at this stage. Even so, among the pilots lost during this first phase of the battle were a significant number who were well tried veterans and sorely missed by their squadrons.

The air fighting over the Channel, or the *Kanalkampf* as the Germans called it, made both sides quickly realise the importance of air-sea rescue for recovering pilots downed in the sea. The Luftwaffe had formed such a service before the war and equipped it with He59 seaplanes and Do18 flying-boats. They carried Red Cross emblems, but were also armed and occurrences of them hovering near British convoys were not infrequent. Consequently the British view was that they were not entitled to the protection of the Red Cross unless they were actually engaged in rescuing aircrew. Consequently a number were shot down by the RAF, which was, in turn, accused of murder by the German propaganda machine. Curiously, the RAF was not well organised in this respect. True, it had had its own high speed launches since the early 1920s – T E Lawrence had served in them during one his spells as an Aircraftsman – but they were slow to realise their value as rescue boats. Not until mid-July did the Air Ministry deploy five launches to the No 11 Group area and ask all Admiralty controlled motor-boats to assist whenever an air battle was taking place in their area. Otherwise, there was just the Royal National Lifeboat Institution. Although the Air-Sea Rescue Service would later become highly organised under RAF Coastal Command, the RAF's early efforts were amateurish and far fewer RAF aircrew were rescued from the Channel than German during the Battle of Britain.

During this first phase of the battle there was only one other Luftwaffe attack on a target other than shipping, besides that on Swansea and Falmouth. This was a night attack by bombers on Merseyside on the night 20/21 July, but little damage resulted. The Straits of Dover, which had become known as 'Stuka Alley', and Dover itself remained the main focus of attention.

On 27 July the port of Dover was subjected to two heavy attacks. The Germans employed a new weapon for these, Me109 fighter-bombers, which came in at almost sea level, even below the CHL radar coverage, and were armed with a 550lb bomb. The Admiralty had already reduced its destroyer strength based there because of previous attacks, but when the first came in at 1430 hours, it took the defences entirely by surprise. Five bombs were dropped, one near miss damaging HMS *Walpole*. The Me109s then climbed into the cloud and headed for home. Just over three hours later came the second attack, again catching the defences out. This time the Me109s were accompanied by Me110s and destroyed HMS *Codrington* by breaking her back. It was clear that it would be madness to try and maintain destroyers here any longer and those that remained, crippled and otherwise, were ordered to Portsmouth. Two days later, the Luftwaffe returned again and destroyed the few remaining ships. The Germans had opened up one invasion route across the Channel. There was also no doubt that they had achieved a degree of supremacy over the Channel and, in recognition of this, the Admiralty ordered that convoys could now only pass down it by night.

It would, however, be wrong to think that the RAF was entirely on the defensive at this time. Throughout July, both by day and by night, RAF Bomber Command attacked targets in Germany, France and the Low Countries. A priority target was invasion

Far left: *A Stuka in action. The centre bomb is 500kg, the others, which were mounted on the wings, 50kg.*

Left: *A Stuka rear gunner boards his aircraft.*

Below: *Stukas of StG77 being armed. The shark's teeth might have helped cause fear on the ground, but did not deter the RAF pilots from inflicting heavy casualties on them.*

barges, which the Germans were now gathering from all over Europe. Airfields, too, in France and Holland were attacked and mines laid around ports.

28 July saw further violent clashes over the Channel. During them one who was to become among the top scoring RAF pilots during the battle, the South African 'Sailor' Malan of 74 Squadron, had the better of a duel with Werner Mölders, forcing him to crash-land. By this stage the British fighter pilots were becoming aware that the tactics that they had been trained on were inferior to those used by the Germans. RAF fighter tactics had been worked out before the war and emphasised, above all else, tight formation flying. The basic formation was the three aircraft section flying in an arrowhead, known as a 'vic', with the section leader in the centre. A squadron airborne would consist of four vics, usually flying line astern, with the squadron commander in the leading vic. When spotting enemy aircraft, the squadron leader ordered one of the laid down 'Fighting Area Attacks'. Each of these had a number and they were executed as standard drills. The first major weakness of this system was that the wingmen in each vic were forced to concentrate so much on keeping formation with their section leader that they did not pay sufficient attention to the rear. Consequently, they could easily be 'bounced' from behind. Furthermore, once the enemy was engaged, the action very quickly generated into a series of dogfights, often individual, in which standard attacks became meaningless.

The Luftwaffe used an entirely different system, one developed by Mölders during the Spanish Civil War. It was based on a unit called a *Schwarm* (flight, or more literally, swarm) made up of two

On 5 September 1940 Oberleutnant Franz von Werra of Jagdgeschwader 3 (below right) *was shot down in his Me109 Emil* (right) *by Flt Lt Paterson Hughes DFC, an Australian with 234 Squadron, himself killed two days later. Von Werra later escaped from a POW camp in Canada and got back to Germany, only to crash and die in the North Sea in 1942. The cutaway drawing* (below) *shows details of the construction of a Bf109E-4 and is depicted in the colours of Von Werra's aircraft.*

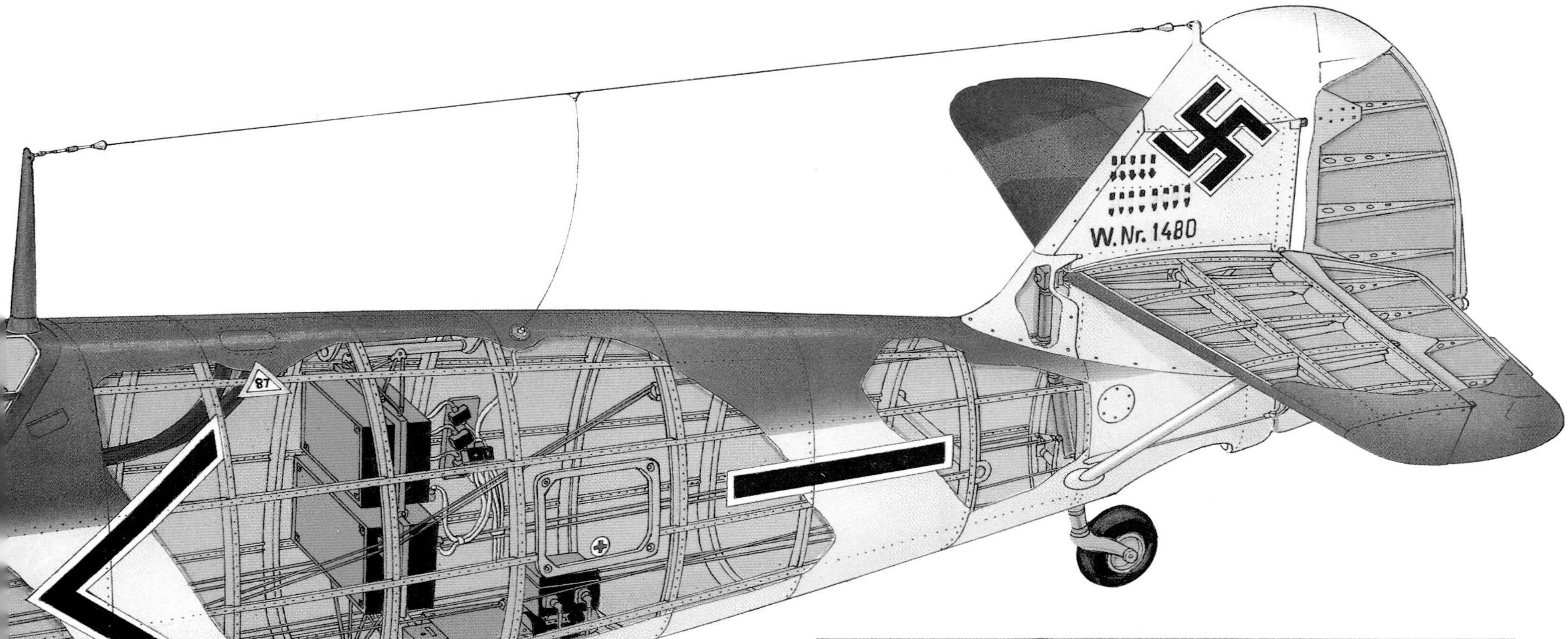

Left: *A Stuka* Staffel *in formation.*

Right: *Coat trailing Me109s off Dover demonstrate the 'finger-four' formation.*

Below: *Repairs under way on the Daimler-Benz 601 engine of an Me109E of JG53.*

pairs (*Rotten*) of aircraft, and known by the RAF as the 'finger-four'. The aircraft in each *Rotte* flew about 200 yards apart and with the No 2 slightly behind the No 1 so that he could cover his rear. Within the *Schwarm* the leader flew slightly ahead of the No 1 of the other *Rotte* and, viewed from above, the formation looked the same as the finger tips of a hand. It was infinitely more flexible and a much better guard against surprise. By the end of the battle a few British squadrons had adopted the system, although it was not officially encouraged. In the meantime, most squadrons used one pilot to fly as 'tail-end Charlie' behind and slightly above the rest of the squadrons in order to guard its rear. This meant much weaving and a danger that he would run out of fuel and so did not really solve the problem. Every fighter pilot, though, was very conscious of his vulnerability to an attack from behind. In this respect his silk scarf, popularly viewed as the fighter pilot's trademark, was by no means mere affectation. The constant head twisting to check the rear could quickly result in a chafed neck, something which silk could prevent. It was a lesson that their fathers had learnt over the Western Front just over twenty years earlier.

The Luftwaffe, too, had learnt some lessons. The Me110 had been shown to be no match for the Spitfire or the Hurricane and the Me109E was not as superior to the Spitfire as had been expected. This was sobering, but the overwhelming belief remained that the Luftwaffe's numerical superiority would achieve the object when the time came. This would not be long now.

On 30 July Hitler ordered Goering to put his *Luftflotten* at twelve hours' notice to begin 'the great battle' against England. Next day he held a conference of his senior commanders at his Alpine retreat at Berchtesgaden. Admiral Raeder warned that the German Navy would not be ready for SEALION until 15 September at the earliest and recommended postponement. This Hitler would not accept since it would merely enable the British Army to be rebuilt. The target date would therefore be 15 September. In the meantime the Luftwaffe was to begin its offensive.

CHAPTER III
EAGLE DAY

Hurricanes of 32 Squadron land at Biggin Hill during the desperate Eagle Day clashes.

Above and right: *Stukas. They attacked their ground targets almost vertically, releasing their bombs and pulling up at the very last moment to ensure accuracy. They were fitted with sirens to create panic.*

Top right: *Paul Nash's famous painting of the Battle of Britain. The contrails were often all that those on the ground saw of the fighting.*

The day after his Berghof conference Hitler issued another directive, No 17, entitled *For the conduct of air and sea warfare against England.* The Luftwaffe's mission was straightforward and unequivocal. 'to overpower the English Air Force with all the forces at its command'. It was to achieve it by attacking 'flying units, their ground installations, and their supply organisations', as well as Britain's aircraft and anti-aircraft equipment industries. Once local air superiority had been achieved the attacks would switch to ports, excluding those on the south coast, which would be needed by the invasion forces, and food stocks. The 'intensification' of the war in the air was to be implemented on or shortly after 5 August, dependent on the progress of preparations and the weather.

The Luftwaffe's appreciation of Britain's air strength in mid-July had concluded that RAF Fighter Command has some 900 fighters, of which 675 were serviceable, but that no more than 300 new fighters at the very maximum could be produced per month. Production would decrease rapidly once the air war intensified. The command structure was viewed as inflexible, although the British pilots were highly regarded. In conclusion the appreciation read: 'The Luftwaffe is clearly superior to the RAF as regards strength, equipment, training, command, and location of bases. In the event of an intensification of air warfare, the Luftwaffe, unlike the RAF, will be in a position, in every respect, to achieve a decisive effect this year.' This general view remained when Goering assembled his commanders at the Hague on the same day that Directive No 17 was issued, 1 August, in order to lay down the concept of operations for what he called *Adlerangriff* (Eagle War).

Goering's plan was for *Luftflotten 2* and *3* to destroy RAF Fighter Command in south-east England. They would do this in three phases. During the first five days radar stations and airfields within a 60-90 mile radius of London would be attacked. This would then be reduced to 30-60 miles for the next three days, and finally to 30 miles for five days. The bombers, besides attacking ground targets would also be used as a bait in order to draw the RAF fighters up. Both Sperrle and Kesselring, as a result of their July experiences, expressed doubts over this. They argued that it would be better for the bombers to attack by night to begin with and only switch to daylight once the RAF aircraft strength had been significantly degraded. Goering, however, would have none of this, believing that RAF Fighter Command had been sufficiently weakened already. The offensive was to be launched on 6 August.

Sperrle and Kesselring were right in their objections. The root of the problem was the limited range of the Me109, the main weapon in the Luftwaffe armoury. Even flying from bases on the Channel coast it only carried sufficient fuel for twenty minutes flying over England and this would be considerably reduced if it had to fight as well. Curiously, the Germans never seem to have considered fitting drop tanks to it and its range limitation would remain a severe disadvantage.

While the Luftwaffe completed their final preparations there was little that the RAF could do but continue its skirmishing and wait for the blow to fall. The Luftwaffe continued its attacks on shipping, but significantly there was an increase in night bomber

raids. On the night of 1/2 August South Wales and the Midlands were attacked. The bombers returned to both regions on the following night, and again on the 3rd/4th before there was a short lull. In each case only a small number of bombers was used and damage was slight. Apart from conservation of strength, the other reason for these small raids was to perfect and train on their *Knickebein* navigation system.

The British had started to become aware that the Germans were developing such a system in March 1940 and by August had learnt sufficient about it to be able to take countermeasures. *Knickebein* meant 'crooked leg' and was evolved from the Lorenz Blind Landing system. By means of a ground transmitter and special Lorenz receiver in the aircraft a pilot could be guided to an airfield and on to the runway simply by listening to the signals he received. *Knickebein* itself used two transmitters, initially at Cleves close to the Dutch border and Brunstedt in Schleswig-Holstein. The idea was that a pilot would pick up one radio beam and fly along it until he met the other beam, which intersected at a point over the target. At the beginning of August the British became aware that new transmitters, smaller than the original two, had been constructed

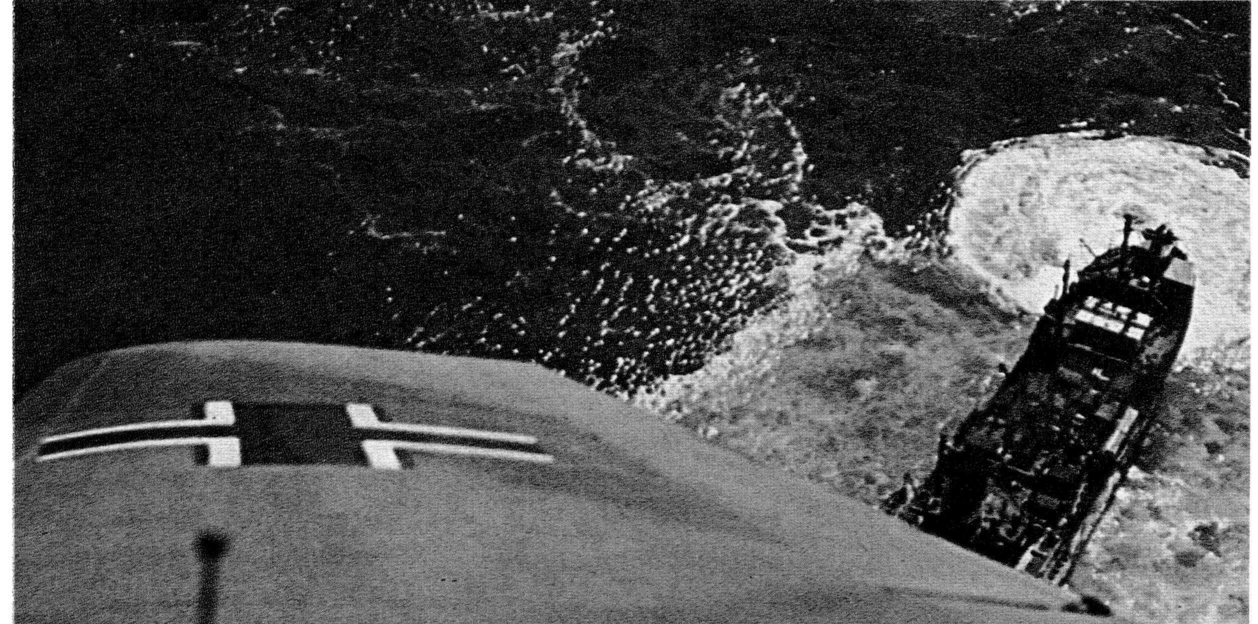

Left: *Dramatic photograph of a Luftwaffe Channel convoy attack. Near miss on a merchant vessel, while the escorting destroyer manoeuvres desperately.*

Typical RAF fighter pilots from 611 Squadron (below left) *and 79 Squadron* (below right). *The man in the black overalls in the latter photograph is a Fleet Air Arm pilot, Sub Lieutenant Joslin, killed in July 1940.*

Left: *He111s maintain a tight formation so that their defensive fire can be mutually supporting.*

Right: *One of the many that did not get home. A crash-landed Me109E somewhere in south-east England, 24 July 1940.*

close to the French coast. They therefore constructed transmitters, codenamed Aspirins, operating on the same frequencies, but sending spurious signals in order to confuse the German bombers and put them off course.

On 6 August Goering laid down that the offensive would begin on the 10th, naming this day *Adlertag*. The past few days had seen relatively little activity, but on the 8th came the largest battle so far. The cause of it was another westbound convoy, CW9, the first for two weeks. Because of the sinkings during July the Admiralty had laid down that convoys would sail by night, laying up in port by day. On 2 August the eastbound Channel convoy CE8 had set sail from Dartmouth on the South Devon case and passed up the Channel without loss. CW9 was to be the return convoy and assembled at Southend on the 6th. Unbeknown to the British, the Germans, using their Freya radars, which were now installed on the French coast, had tracked CE8, and were ready for CW9, which passed through the Straits of Dover in the late afternoon of the 7th. That night it was attacked by E-boats, which torpedoed three coasters and caused two others to collide. Two destroyers were despatched from Portsmouth to sort out the resultant chaos.

Although they managed to drive off the E-boats, it was impossible to reorganise the convoy and dawn arrived with the ships still at sea.

This was too good a target to ignore and the Stukas were soon out in force. RAF fighters were sent up and additional Me109s until there were over 150 aircraft scrapping over the Channel. The result was that 31 German aircraft, including eight Stukas, who were beginning to reveal their vulnerability, and 20 RAF fighters were lost. As for the convoy, two further ships were sunk and many more damaged.

The next two days were comparatively quiet, largely because of cloud and rain. As a result of this Goering made a number of postponements to *Adlertag*. On the 11th there was an improvement in the weather and the day dawned fine. German attacks were made on Dover and the naval bases at Weymouth and Portland. The total of aircraft engaged was even higher than on the 8th. The margin of losses was also much closer, 38 German against 32 RAF. On this day Goering decided, having been told that the spell of fine weather would last for some days, that Eagle Day would definitely be 13 August. As a necessary preliminary there would be attacks on the south coast radar stations, which, because of their high masts, were easy to spot. There would be dealt with on the 12th and Goering himself would be present in person on the French Channel coast to observe the attacks.

The first strike against Chain Home was timed for 0910 hours and would be carried out by a special unit *Eroberungsgruppe* (Conquest Group) *210* led by Captain Walter Rubensdörffer. This was equipped with bomb carrying Me109s and Me110s which specialised in tackling difficult precision targets and had already been in action on 29 July in the attacks on Dover. For the attacks on the radar stations Rubensdörffer employed sixteen Me110s in four sections. One led by himself would attack the station at Dunkirk,

north-west of Dover, while the others took on the stations at Pevensey, Rye and Dover itself. All four stations were hit and it seemed from subsequent reports that the attack had been almost wholly successful. Certainly, during the next few hours several coat trailing Me109s appeared over the Kent and Sussex coasts and even though RAF fighters were on standing patrol in the area no contacts were made. The damage was, however, less than it seemed. The crucial elements of the station were constructed of reinforced concrete and they and the radar masts survived the attacks with just a temporary disruption to communications.

Kesselring also sent Stukas to attack shipping in the Thames Estuary and North Foreland, but these were picked up by the CHL station at Foreness. Fighters, some already airborne, were sent to intercept. Over the Thames Estuary the RAF failed to get in amongst the Stukas before being attacked by their escorting Me109s, but between Deal and Ramsgate they had better success, shooting down four Ju87s.

The main attacks of the day were made further west along the coast. Among the targets were the naval bases at Portsmouth and Portland, factories at Portsmouth and Southampton, and the vital radar station at Ventnor in the Isle of Wight. No less than one hundred Ju88s escorted by 120 Me110s and 25 Me109s were allocated for these. Because of the earlier disruption caused to Chain Home it was not functioning as it should, it was only the eyes of the Royal Observer Corps posts that picked up the attackers as they flew across the Channel. Over fifty RAF fighters were scrambled, most flying towards Portsmouth. This was a correct decision, for it was against this port that the Ju88s initially concentrated. Some, however, led by Colonel Dr Fisser, commander of KG51, turned off towards the Isle of Wight and struck the Ventnor radar station, putting it out of action. As he turned away after the attack Fisser's Ju88 was attacked by Spitfires which killed him and forced his air-

Opposite top: *Flight Lieutenant Rhodes Moorhouse DFC, son of a World War I Royal Flying Corps VC.*

Opposite bottom: *616 Squadron pilots. Three would be dead and one a POW before the Battle ended.*

Above: *David Crook, one of the top pilots in 609 Squadron.*

Below: *74 Squadron, Manston, July 1940.*

craft to crash-land on English soil. The battle over Portsmouth went on for some time, with anti-aircraft and ship's guns joining in the fray before the raiders turned for home.

The Luftwaffe was by no means finished for the day. In the afternoon they struck RAF airfields, the three that happened to be nearest to the coast. Lympne had already been attacked earlier in the day. It was to be visited by the RAF's Inspector General, Sir Edgar Ludlow-Hewitt, in the early evening, and the station commander was concerned to have the damage cleared up before he arrived. As it happened, his arrival coincided with that of the Ju88s and he was bundled into a shelter while they, and a second wave of Do17s, plastered the airfield from end to end. Hawkinge suffered the same, as did Manston.

Manston itself, which was probably the most frequently attacked airfield during the battle, was the home of 600 Squadron, which flew Blenheims in the nightfighter role. Fighter squadrons, however, used it by day. When attacked it so happened that 65 Squadron, with its 12 Spitfires, was just taking off. Miraculously, eleven of the twelve made it, and the Me109s which then attacked them overshot because the Spitfires had only just attained flying speed.

This attack was the beginning of what developed into a scurrilous myth, that of the so-called Manston Mutiny. The ground crews, so the myth went, refused to rearm and refuel visiting fighters, leaving 600 Squadron's aircrews to do it. The ground crews themselves are supposed to have remained cowering in the shelters for the next ten days, refusing to come out and go back on duty. This was totally untrue. What in fact happened was that after the raid some 250 RAF recruits were sent from Blackpool to help fill in the numerous craters. Their NCOs immediately returned by train to Blackpool. On arrival at the airfield there was an air raid alarm and they were ordered to go to the shelters. In the confusion of the repeated attacks on Manston, the wretched recruits were forgotten about and were only discovered three days later, their morale now shattered, and were returned to Blackpool. The ground crews themselves continued to display the utmost devotion to duty and, on 22 August, received a signal from Keith Park congratulating them on their steadfastness.

If 12 August was to be a foretaste of what was to come then Dowding and his Group Commanders, especially Park, had cause for concern. True, four of the Chain Home stations and their communications were working again before the day was out (Ventnor would take three days to repair), but the system could not survive against repeated attack. Likewise, if all Fighter Command airfields in southern England were subjected to prolonged attack it would be difficult to prevent the Luftwaffe from achieving air superiority, especially if Chain Home was rendered inoperative as well. Dowding knew from a decrypted Enigma exhortatory message from Goering to his *Luftflotten* that next day was to be the beginning of *Adlerangriff*.

As it happened, the 13th began cloudy, but at 0500 Dorniers of KG2 and their escorting Me110s of ZG26 began to take off, their destination Eastchurch and Sheerness. Just as they were forming up over the Channel Goering sent a radio message calling the attack off. He wanted to delay it until later in the day because of the cloud. The fighters received the message, but the bombers did not because, for some reason, they did not have the right crystals in their sets. They continued on to their targets. Although the Chain Home stations spotted them they lost track of the bombers and cloud prevented the Royal Observer Corps from picking them up. Even so, three fighter squadrons were able to intercept, shot down five Do17s and badly damaged six more before the bombers reached their target. Nevertheless, Eastchurch airfield was hit and a 266 Squadron Spitfire destroyed on the ground.

It was not until mid-afternoon that the main attack was launched. Almost 300 aircraft from Sperrle's Luftflotte 3 assem-

Far left: *The Operations Room at HQ Fighter Command.*

Left: *Ginger Lacey, top scoring RAF pilot during the Battle, who died in 1989.*

Below left: *Tom Gleave, CO of 253 Squadron, and one of plastic surgeon Archibald McIndoe's 'Guinea Pigs'.*

Below right: *Flt Lt 'Sammy' Allard DFC DFM, 85 Squadron.*

bled over the Cherbourg peninsula and then set course for No 10 Group's airfields and Southampton. They were preceded by Me109s designed to tempt the British fighters into the air so that they would be out of fuel by the time that the main force arrived. It did not work in this case. The centre of Southampton was badly damaged, as were the docks. The Stukas' efforts to find Warmwell and Middle Wallop, which housed a sector control room, were, however, in vain and one *Staffel* lost six of its nine aircraft to the guns of 609 Squadron's Spitfires.

Sperrle had failed to knock out No 10 Group, but Kesselring still had some cards to play against No 11 Group. He sent two groups of Stukas to destroy the airfields at Rochester and Detling. The Rochester group failed to find their target and met 56 Squadron instead. This was not the case at Detling, which happened to be a Coastal Command airfield, and the damage was considerable. No less than 22 aircraft were destroyed on the ground and the station commander killed. This ended an otherwise frustrating Eagle Day for the Germans on a high note. None the less they had lost 45 aircraft shot down and three others from other causes. Several others had been badly damaged. On the other side of the balance sheet the RAF's losses were 13 aircraft and three pilots. At the time, though, the Air Ministry claimed that 78 German aircraft had been shot down while the Germans believed that the losses were 5:1 in their favour. This was partly propaganda, but also because it was often difficult during those hectic days to verify claims. On the British side every effort was made to confirm 'kills' by the use of witnesses, air and ground, but this was often difficult during the confused mêlée that much of the air fighting was and it was understandable that pilots were optimistic over their claims. For the Germans the task was even more difficult since they were not in a position to check on their victims shot down over England. However, unlike the British, who would share out a victory if more than one aircraft was involved, the Germans tended to award a 'kill' to each pilot, which, of course, did significantly inflate the total.

During the night German bombers attacked the Spitfire factory in Birmingham, causing slight damage, and the Short Brothers factory in Belfast, where five Stirling 4-engine bombers under construction were destroyed. In return RAF Bomber Command attacked Italy for the first time, with Whitleys bombing targets in Milan and Turin.

14 August was a day of cloud with bright periods over England. Little happened until midday when a big clash developed in the Dover area involving upwards of 200 aircraft. Rubensdörffer's Me110s struck Manston again, but lost two of their number to ground fire. Sperrle, on the other hand, contented himself with a number of three-aircraft raids on airfields. One trio of He111s even attacked an airfield in Cheshire, and others bombed Middle Wallop causing some damage. That evening Dowding relieved three of the most tired squadrons, sending them up to No 13 Group to refurbish.

On 15 August the Luftwaffe played a new card. *Luftflotte* 5 was employed for the first time. This was in the mistaken belief that all the RAF's fighters were in the south and that the north of England was therefore undefended. As it was, Dowding had resisted

Above right: *John Dundas (609 Sqn) was killed in the Battle. His equally famous brother Hugh ('Cocky') fought with 616 Squadron and survived the war.*

Right: *Downed Ju88. Shot down aircraft often revealed valuable technical intelligence.*

Above: *'Johnny Head in the Air' – Hurricane pilot. Note how he wore his parachute, which he would sit on when in his cockpit.*

Left: *'A' Flight pilots of 17 Squadron at Debden in No 11 Group's area, July 1940. Left to right, Flying Officer Hanson, Flight Lieutenant Harper, Pilot Officer Bennette, F/O Stevens, F/O Pittman, Sgt Griffiths.*

temptation to do this for the same reason that he had argued against fighter squadrons being sent to France. The Luftwaffe plan did not work. *Luftflotte 5* could not use its Me109s because the distance across the North Sea was too great, although some Me110s with belly mounted drop tanks did accompany the 65 He111s from Norway. The fifty Ju88s from Denmark had to rely on their own armament. Picked up by radar in good time, both groups clashed with Spitfires and Hurricanes of Nos 12 and 13 Groups and the result was almost a massacre. Twenty-two German aircraft fell from the skies and others were badly damaged. All they had to show for this was ten Whitley bombers destroyed on the ground at Driffield, a blown up ammunition dump, some 30 houses damaged in Sunderland and Bridlington, and one damaged Hurricane forced to return early to base.

Luftflotten 2 and *3* hoped to attack at the same time as Stumpff, but cloud prevented this and their attacks did not begin until the early afternoon. Stukas struck both Lympne and Manston again and suffered further damage, but fighters intercepted another lunge at Hawkinge, shooting down two Stukas and damaging others before top cover Me109s shot down four of the defenders. Martlesham Heath was also hit by Rubensdörffer's Me109 and Me110 fighter-bombers. This was just a preliminary.

The plotting boards in the control rooms now showed an ominous build up of German aircraft over Normandy and the Cherbourg peninsula. These carried out a number of simultaneous raids against Portsmouth, Southampton, Weymouth, Portland and various airfields. No less than fourteen 10 and 11 Group squadrons were scrambled to meet this multi-threat. Desperate battles followed, with casualties heavy on both sides. As the fighting subsided another substantial plot began to develop over the Pas de Calais. This was KG3 with 90 Dorniers and escorted by no less than 130 Me109s. In addition, 60 coat trailing Me109s preceded the attack. The targets were Eastchurch and an aircraft factory at Rochester. Both were hit and the Short Brothers factory badly damaged. Only three squadrons could be directed onto this massive force and they made little impression, shooting down two bombers, but losing significantly more of their own. And this was still not the end.

Kesselring launched two more attacks shortly after 1800 hours. Airfields were the target once again. Dorniers with an Me109 escort were directed to Biggin Hill while Rubensdörffer and his fighter-bombers were to strike at Kenley. The Dorniers failed to find Biggin Hill, and dropped their bombs on an unfinished airfield

Above: *No 1 (RCAF) Squadron Hurricane jacked up for inspection.*

Below: *The New Zealander Al Deere (right), one of the leading RAF fighter pilots. 1943 photograph.*

Top right: *Cheerful 54 Squadron pilots. Based at Hornchurch this squadron was in the front line for much of the Battle and was sent north to Yorkshire for a rest at the beginning of September.*

at West Malling. Rubensdörffer's navigation was also letting him down and he attacked Croydon instead. The No 11 Group controllers had, however, guessed that Kenley would be his target and 111 Squadron, whose home Croydon was, had been sent up and contacted the Me110s as they attacked the airfield. Aircraft from 32 Squadron at Biggin Hill soon joined them. Six Me110s were sent to the ground, one of them Rubensdörffer's, shot down appropriately by 111 Squadron's commander, John Thompson.

This day had seen the heaviest fighting in the battle so far, with the Luftwaffe mounting no less than 1750 sorties. In all 75 Luftwaffe aircraft failed to return, although at the time the British claimed 144 shot down, but 34 RAF fighters had been lost, together with 13 pilots killed and three made prisoner, having landed or been forced down on the wrong side of the Channel. For the Germans the day had been one of disappointment, but it had stretched Fighter Command to the utmost. General 'Pug' Ismay, Churchill's military link with the Chiefs of Staff, had spent the day at HQ No 11 Group and recorded: 'There had been heavy fighting throughout the afternoon and at one moment every single squadron in the group was engaged; there was nothing in reserve, and the map table showed new waves of attackers crossing the coast. I felt sick with fear.'

The next day was to bring no respite. The action began in mid-morning with Dorniers making another attack on the incomplete field at West Malling. A more sizeable attack developed over the Kent coast at midday and Park put up some 80 fighters to meet it. This was sufficient to ward the bombers away from their prime target, the station at Hornchurch, but at a cost in the loss of more experienced pilots. Within the hour *Luftflotte 3* made its first attack, designed to catch No 11 Group while they were still refueling and rearming after *Luftflotte 2's* attack. The station at Tangmere was badly damaged in a Stuka attack, with six Blenheims and seven Hurricanes destroyed. 43 Squadron shot down seven of the raiders on their way home and ground fire accounted for another. Flight Lieutenant James Nicholson of 249 Squadron had his section bounced by Me109s, which shot down one Hurricane. He himself, his aircraft on fire, engaged and shot down one of the attackers before baling out with severe hand and face burns. He was awarded the only Victoria Cross won during the battle by RAF Fighter Command.

There was then a short lull until 1630 hours, when further raids began. By now cloud had arrived, which made interception much more difficult and the Luftwaffe was able to attack targets with relative impunity. The most serious was that by two Ju88s against RAF Brize Norton in Oxfordshire. This was a training base and maintenance unit. No less than 46 Airspeed Oxford trainers were destroyed, and 11 Hurricanes undergoing repair were also damaged.

As well as Nicholson's VC, two VCs were won by Bomber Command personnel during the period of the Battle. Flight Lieutenant 'Babe' Learoyd was awarded his for his courage and skill in a low level attack on the Dortmund-Ems Canal in his badly damaged

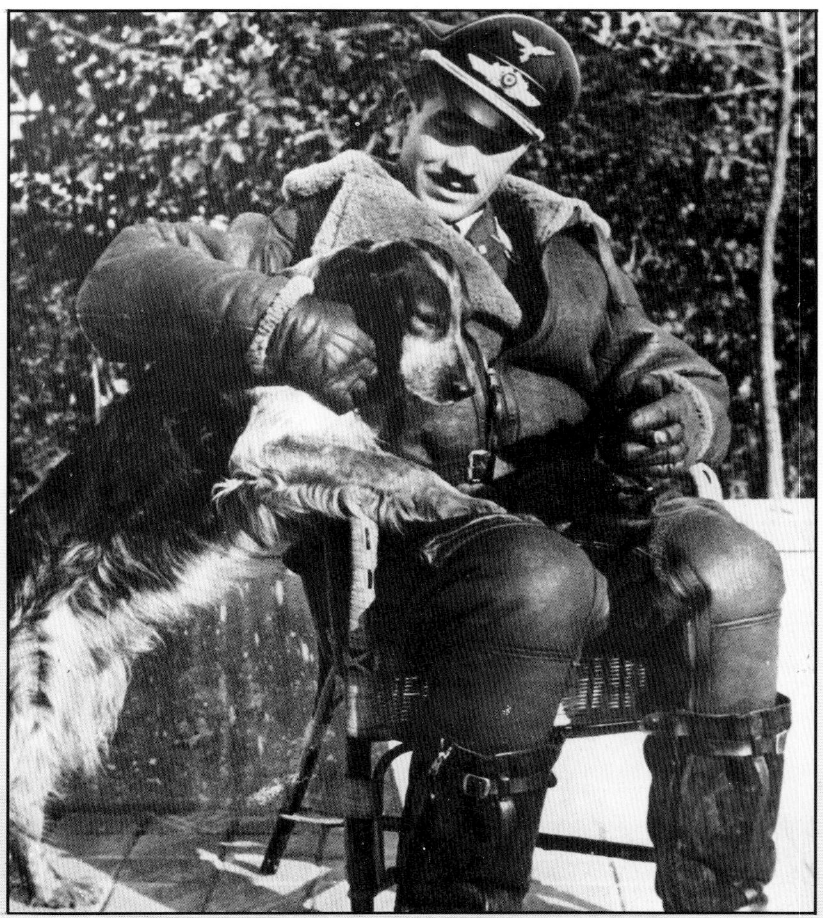

Far left: *A Ju88 nose gunner prepares for a night mission.*

Left: *German ace Adolf Galland.*

Right: *Death of an He111.*

Below: *He111s en route to their target.*

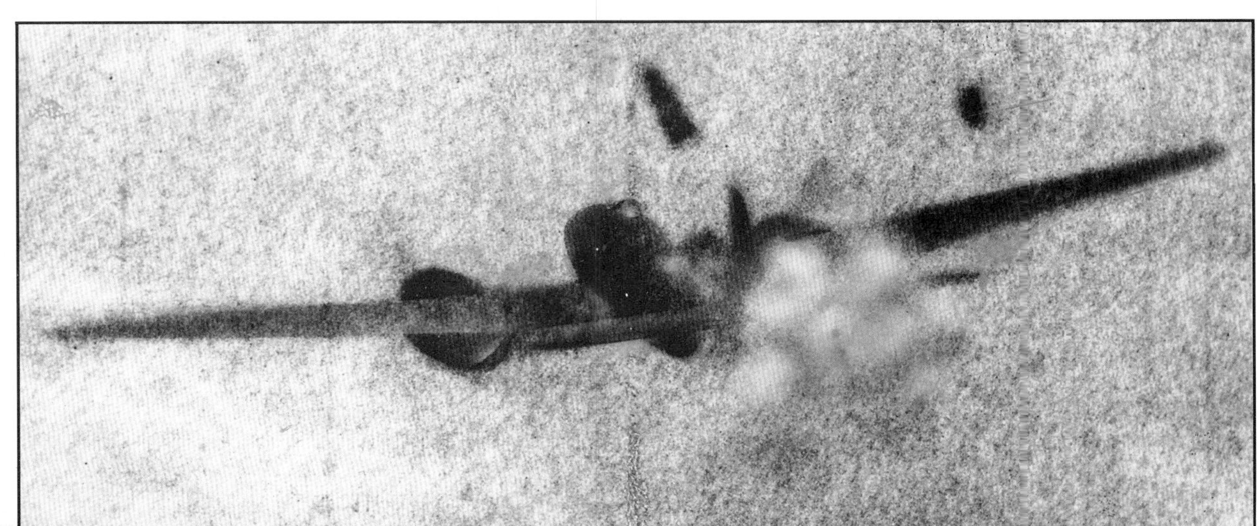

Hampden on the night of 12/13 August, while Sergeant John Hannah won his in another Hampden. The aircraft was hit by flak and set on fire during an attack on barges in the Antwerp docks on the night of 15/16 September. Hannah, although badly burned, successfully fought the fire and the Hampden got back to base.

After a pause on 17 August, during which the RAF was able to do much to repair the bomb craters and communications damage to its front line airfields, battle was joined again on 18 August. The airfield at Kenley was attacked first by low flying Dorniers and then, a few minutes later, by Ju88s. The Dorniers created much damage, and virtually severed all communications to and from the ops room, which miraculously survived. Even so, the defenders were ready and employed a new weapon. This was a system called Parachute and Cable (PAC), by which rockets fired 500ft of cable into the air. Parachutes opened on it allowing it to sink slowly to earth. PAC accounted for at least two of the Dorniers and ground fire for another, before fighters fell on the others and harried them all the way home. The Ju88s added to the damage, bombing from 12,000ft, but six Hurricanes managed to disrupt their formation as they began to make their bombing runs and this meant that a good proportion of the bombs missed the target. Biggin Hill was subjected to the same treatment, but the damage was much less. PAC accounted for two Dorniers and five others of the nine which made very low level attacks were hacked down by fighters on their way back. In the aftermath, a member of the Women's Auxiliary Air Force, Sergeant Joan Mortimer, was awarded the Military

Above: *Ground crew put in a maximum effort to get this 19 Squadron Spitfire ready for the next scramble.*

Top right: *Hurricane prepares to taxi prior to take-off.*

Right: *A D Nesbilt, a member of I (RCAF) Squadron during the Battle. Photograph taken in 1942.*

Medal for her coolness in marking unexploded bombs. Two other WAAF's would be similarly honoured for remaining at their posts at the station's telephone switchboard during a later heavy attack on Biggin Hill. Croydon and West Malling were also attacked, receiving slight damage.

The afternoon saw further attacks in the Portsmouth-Southampton area. The radar station at Poling and the airfield at Ford were badly hit by Stukas, but fighters caught the Ju87s as they were preparing to strike RAF Canvey Island and caused much carnage among them. Indeed, this marked the end of the Stuka's role in the battle. No less than thirty of them were shot down or severely damaged, one *Gruppe* losing half the aircraft it had sent out.

Many commentators have called 18 August the toughest day of the battle. The losses on each side were very similar to those on the 15th, but the damage caused to RAF Fighter Command's infrastructure was much greater. What was especially serious was that since the beginning of August 106 RAF fighter pilots had been killed and many others badly injured. The Operational Training Units (OTU) had up until now still been carrying on as in peacetime and were only supplying about one third of the replacement pilots needed. In desperation Fighter Command had borrowed pilots from the other commands and even from the Fleet Air Arm in order to make good the shortage.

By this stage the pilots of Fighter Command were from a wide range of countries other than Britain itself From within the British Empire the New Zealanders led the way, with no less than

129 taking part in the battle. These included the legendary Alan Deere and Colin Gray. There was a strong contingent of Canadians. A number had fought in 242 Squadron in France and remained in the squadron under Douglas Bader, the legless British ace. The first RCAF squadron to see action in the war, 1 (later 401) Squadron, was also involved in the battle. South Africans, Rhodesians and a Jamaican also fought. There were also seven Americans, one of whom, Billy Fiske, died of injuries received in the fighting of 16 August. There was also a large contingent from the countries overrun by Hitler. This was led by the Poles, many of whom had experienced extraordinary adventures to get to England, and whose desire for vengeance gave them a unique aggressiveness in the air. Many Czech pilots took part, including Josef Frantisek, who, when he was killed on 8 October 1940, was the top scoring pilot in the command, with 28 victories to his credit. Belgians and Frenchmen also distinguished themselves. At times some squadrons had a complete mix of these nationalities, although Polish and Czech squadrons were formed. Many of the 'refugees' were highly experienced pilots.

To the relief of the aircrews of both sides the weather now decided to take a hand. Cloud and rain dramatically reduced the intensity of operations over the period 19-23 August. For the Germans this was an opportunity to rethink their tactics and for the RAF time to try and make good the ravages of the past days. Two significant but simple improvements were being made to the British fighters at this time. The first was some armour protection for the pilots, consisting of a slab being fitted behind their seats. The other, and it is extraordinary that no one had thought of it before, was the installation of a rear view mirror in the cockpit. The part being played by the RAF's fighter pilots was, in the meantime publicly recognised by Prime Minister Winston Churchill in the House of Commons on 20 August in those now immortal words: 'Never in the field of human conflict was so much owed by so many to so few.'

Left: *Heroines of the WAAF. Left to Right – Joan Mortimer, Elspeth Henderson and Emily Turner, who were awarded the Military Medal for bravery during the Luftwaffe attacks on Biggin Hill.*

Right: *Another New Zealand ace, Bill Crawford-Compton DSO DFC.*

Below: *A group of largely Australian pilots, recognisable by their darker blue uniforms.*

CHAPTER IV

THE POUNDING CONTINUES

Children being evacuated from London's East End.

Above: *Part of London's anti-aircraft defences in action. The YMCA mobile tea bar plays its part.*

Right: *7 September 1940. An oil refinery at Purfleet in the Essex marshes by the Thames under Luftwaffe attack.*

Top right: *An old ace compares notes with the new aces. (Left to right) Wilhelm Balthasar, Walter Oesau, Adolf Galland, General Udet, Werner Mölders, unidentified, Hartmann Grasser.*

Goering summoned his senior commanders to two meetings at his country retreat, Karinhall, on 15 and 19 August. He was both disappointed and frustrated that the RAF seemed to be fighting as strongly as ever in spite of the casualties that had been inflicted on it. He reserved his venom for the Me109 pilots whom he accused of showing lack of aggression. There was a purge among their heirarchy, with Mölders and Galland each being promoted to command a Geschwader. From now on, Goering declared, the primary objective was the destruction of the RAF fighter force. 'If they no longer take to the air, we shall attack them on the ground, or force them into battle by directing bomber attacks against targets within range of air fighters.' In effect, the bombers were to be used as mere bait. *Luftflotte 2* would take on this task by day and would concentrate on No 11 Group, while *Luftflotte 3* would carry out the night raids. Other measures were instituted. The Me110s would no longer be deployed without Me109s, unless the target was beyond the range of the latter. The Stukas were to be conserved for the invasion, with just two *Staffeln* being left with *Luftflotte 2* for use against pinpoint targets, but only where local air supremacy had been gained. Goering also laid down that on operations no more than one commissioned officer per aircraft would be allowed. Too many had been lost during the past few weeks. Finally, he declared that Chain Home stations were not to be attacked because of the difficulty of knocking them out. This was defeatism and ignored the success against Ventnor and Poling. It would prove to be a critical error of judgement.

Although he had been destroying twice as many enemy aircraft as Fighter Command had lost, Dowding remained deeply concerned. The Luftwaffe had substantial reserves while he had few. Furthermore, he was well aware that the men and women of his command were becoming desperately tired. Life on the front line airfields was very tough. The ground crews struggled desperately to keep their aircraft in the air, but also found themselves having to help fill in bomb craters after raids. Bomb damage disrupted catering arrangements and the long hours they had to work meant little sleep. The pilots, too, were suffering increasing strain. The tensions of waiting for the telephone to ring in the dispersal hut, what one pilot called 'telephoneitis', the intense excitement of the scramble, the dryness in the mouth when the enemy was contacted, the pumping of adrenalin that combat brought, all added to the stress. Indeed, one station medical officer later likened aircrew to a spring. Every operation represented the spring being compressed to expand again on landing. After a time the spring began to tire and took increasingly longer to expand and eventually cracked. At this time there were no laid down tour lengths and pilots were just expected to fly on until they could not take any more and then it was up to the squadron commander to decide whether to rest them. Because of the shortage of pilots – Fighter Command was almost 400 under establishment by the August lull – and the increasing proportion of new pilots, many of whom had had less than ten hours on Spitfires or Hurricanes before they arrived in their squadrons, and who needed a chance to get accli-

Right: *Captured Luftwaffe aircrew are escorted through London.*

Far right: *An He111 nose gunner watches anxiously for RAF fighters.*

Bottom row, left: *Downed Me110 being prepared for public display.*

Bottom row, centre: *He111 crews enjoy an alfresco lunch, an indication of the intensity of operations.*

Bottom row, right: *The ideal position – an He111 comes into range of an RAF fighter's guns.*

matised before being committed to combat, squadron commanders were understandably loath to let the 'old hands' go. All that could be done was to exchange tired squadrons with fresh ones from No 13 Group, but this only provided a partial answer. During the lull Dowding was able to exchange four squadrons in this way.

The lull itself was not a total one. Me109s continued to try and provoke their opposite numbers, making 'tip and run' raids on airfields. By night, too, the bombers continued active, their targets mainly aircraft factories, but not always. Towns and cities as far north as Aberdeen were attacked, as was South Wales, Liverpool, Birmingham and the Kent ports. The Blenheim nightfighter crews, with their then very primitive radar air interception sets, had little success at this time, with one inconclusive engagement in 160 sorties.

On 24 August improved weather heralded the resumption of the main battle. Manston, North Weald and Hornchurch were hammered and once again Park's resources were sorely stretched, even though he had issued orders that his fighters were not to tangle with their own kind unless they had to, but must make their priority the bombers. Although Sperrle's main role was now night attacks, he still launched an attack in the afternoon – the old idea of catching No 11 Group refuelling after Kesselring's attacks. This time Portsmouth was the victim, and, because Ventnor was still not properly functioning, no RAF fighters were able to intercept the raiders before they attacked. The damage to the city and its port was considerable.

That night bombs landed on London for the first time. At the time it seemed as though the treatment that had been meted out to Warsaw and Rotterdam was now to be inflicted on the capital. In fact, Goering had issued strict instructions that London was not to be attacked without his permission, which had not yet been given, and it was a navigational error on the part of the crew that did so. The consequences of this would be wide ranging.

On the 25th there was no significant activity until mid afternoon. The main action was over Portland and Weymouth and the target the air base at Warmwell. RAF fighters succeeded in intercepting the raiders before they reached their target and preventing many of them from getting through to it, but one bomb did cut all the airfield's communications. More worrying was that 16 RAF aircraft were shot down, but only 20 German. This marked the beginning of a disturbing new trend, largely brought about by the higher concentration of escorting Me109s, in which the margin of losses on each side significantly narrowed.

That night, on Churchill's express orders, RAF Bomber Command attacked Berlin for the first time. The 81 aircraft that took off had orders to bomb industrial targets on the outskirts of the city. Heavy cloud resulted in only 29 claiming to have attacked, and the damage was negligible, with no civilian casualties. The cloud, however, protected the bombers from flak and all returned safely. It made nonsense of Goering's proud boast that no British bomber would ever get through to Berlin, but it was inevitable that the Germans would retaliate. The next few nights saw attacks on Merseyside. While the hard working Aspirins were able to deflect many of the bombers by interfering with *Knickebein*, on the 31st Liverpool was badly hit, with no less than 160 fires being started in its commercial centre. In its turn, the RAF made further small attacks on Berlin and other German towns and cities. Then, on 4 September,

Left: *A Czech Hurricane pilot greets his squadron's mascot on return from a sortie.*

Below left: *Irish fighter ace Paddy Finucane. Note the shamrock emblem.*

Bottom left: *Ronald Hamlyn, who had five victories during one day in August 1940.*

Hitler told a rally of nurses and social workers in Berlin: 'When the British Air Force drops two or three or four thousand kilograms of bombs, then we will in one night drop 150, 230, 300 or 400 thousand kilograms. When they declare that they will increase their attacks on our cities, then we will *raze* their cities to the ground. We will stop the handiwork of these night air pirates, so help us God!' The era of area bombing or 'city busting', as it was also called, was about to arrive.

Meanwhile the No 11 Group airfields continued to be pulverised, and Park's efforts to avoid the German fighters and concentrate on the bombers were often frustrated. Apart from the increased numbers of Me109s, they also had orders to escort the bombers more closely and hence it was more difficult to avoid them. Furthermore, the No 11 Group squadrons were invariably heavily outnumbered because Park could not afford to put them into the air all at once for fear of them being caught refuelling and rearming when the next attack came. Consequently, he always had to maintain a sizeable reserve on the ground.

The perspective of No 12 Group to Park's north was very different. Their prime role was to guard the Midlands, and their secondary role to reinforce Park where necessary. Because of Dowding's careful husbanding of his slender resources Leigh-Mallory's squadrons often found themselves frustrated bystanders to the desperate battles going on to their south. No one was more frustrated than Leigh-Mallory himself, who was not only jealous of Park's role, but also disagreed fundamentally with Dowding's tactics. Indeed, according to Park, as early as March 1940, Leigh-Mallory had vowed to move heaven and earth to get Dowding sacked.

Douglas Bader, too, commanding 242 Squadron at Coltishall was chafing at the bit. He firmly believed in the principles of air fighting evolved by the McCuddens, Balls, Mannocks and Bishops during World War 1. In essence this was to achieve height over the enemy, to attack with the sun behind and to get in close before opening fire. Too often, he thought, squadrons were not scram-

Right: *Bob Stanford-Tuck who led 257 Squadron with dash and verve.*

Below right: *Two of 85 Squadron's leading pilots, R H A Lee DSO DFC and A G Lewis DFC.*

bled in time enough to achieve height and their piecemeal commitment made the disparity in numbers even greater than need be. Rather, he argued, fighters should be committed as 'wings' of three, four, or even five squadrons operating together. If the 12 Group squadrons were sent aloft in this way as soon as an attack was detected by 11 Group they could achieve the necessary height and position to wreak real damage on the enemy. His ideas were reinforced by an experience he had on 30 August. Park's tactic was to call on 12 Group squadrons to protect his more northerly airfields when a raid was in progress. Bader was ordered by the 12 Group controller to orbit North Weald at 15,000ft. Bader considered this unsatisfactory and positioned himself away from the airfield with the sun behind him. As it was, he located the German bombers and attacked, shooting a number down without loss. In contrast, another 12 Group squadron which was sent to Biggin Hill failed to make contact and the airfield was badly damaged. That evening he spoke to Leigh-Mallory, who agreed that Bader could try out his ideas. The fact that he should have referred this radical proposal to Dowding does not seem to have occurred to Leigh-Mallory, perhaps an indication of his low opinion of the AOCinC.

This was the origin of what became knows as the Duxford Wing, consisting of Bader's squadron and 19 and 310 (Czech) Squadrons from Duxford. During the next few days Bader practised scrambling his three squadrons and was able to achieve a time of six minutes between the alert being sounded and his 36 aircraft being in the sky and in formation. All he required from the controllers was the height of the enemy aircraft and their direction of flight. He would then decide where to position himself. The problem about this was that it cut across Dowding's whole principle of centralised control, which he saw as the only way in which his resources could be most effectively used against the enemy. It also complicated Park's problems in that the 12 Group squadrons operating in this way in his area were difficult to control. Most serious was that it inevitably cut across the principle of engaging the bombers before they reached their target, since by the time Bader had positioned himself to his satisfaction they would already be turning for home. The 12 Group riposte to this was that it was better to destroy 50 aircraft after they had bombed than ten before they did so. It was not an argument that cut much ice with Park, struggling as he was to maintain his battered infrastructures, but, in any event, it was not until the next phase of the battle that the Duxford Wing would have a real opportunity to show what it could do.

The attacks on No 11 Group's airfields were unceasing over this period. As Park later wrote: 'Contrary to general belief and official reports, the enemy's bombing attacks did extensive damage to five of our forward aerodromes and also to six of our seven sector stations.' While there was a system of satellite airfields, often just grass strips, squadrons could not divorce themselves from their normal bases for more than a day or so, because the satellites lacked the essential workshops and other facilities needed to keep the aircraft properly maintained. Likewise, there were emergency control rooms, often camouflaged in houses and shops. These, however, lacked some of the necessary communications to ensure good command and control. As it was, those responsible for maintaining communications links, the Post Office (for the peacetime

telephone system), RAF Signals Branch and Royal Signals, often found themselves working round the clock. Even so, Park made the point about the damage caused during the last week of August and the first in September that 'there was a critical period when the damage to the sector stations and our ground organisation was having a serious effect on the fighting efficiency of the squadrons'.

Another major cause for concern was that for the first time the loss of fighter aircraft was exceeding production. Over the period 24 August – 6 September RAF Fighter Command lost a total of 295 Hurricanes and Spitfires, with another 171 badly damaged. Production output, including fighters repaired, over the same period was only 269, a serious shortfall. Worse, the Luftwaffe resumed its attacks on aircraft factories on 2 September. Shorts at Rochester was hit again as was the Vickers factory at Brooklands, where Wellington bombers were being produced. Nearby, however, was a Hurricane factory, and this was hit on the 5th. Luckily the damage was only slight. But, even if the Luftwaffe continued to miss the fighter factories and the attrition rate stayed the same it was calculated that another three weeks were all that was needed for Goering to achieve his aim.

Happily the British people were largely unaware of the growing crisis. The newspapers gave highly optimistic daily scores of aircraft shot down, encouraging the public to view the contest as a sport. Newsboys chalked up on the boards such headlines as 'BIGGEST RAID EVER – SCORE 78 TO 26 – ENGLAND STILL BATTING'. The bravery of the fighter pilots was widely acknowledged and an aura of glamour built up around them, which caused those in other services and RAF commands to dub them the 'Brylcream Boys', after a popular hair lotion of the day. Yet, the general belief was that they were naturally superior to their German counterparts, as were their aircraft, and this provided a warm cocoon against the increasing seriousness of the true situation.

Those living in south-east and southern England had, of course, a grandstand view of what was going on. Often, if the fighting was at altitude all that could be seen were the contrails of the aircraft and the distant sound of guns. Occasionally an aircraft would be seen falling to earth, as well as the odd parachute. At low level life was more hair raising, as one fighter pursued another, with its guns firing, screamed over at treetop height, the bullets knocking slates off roofs and causing the odd casualty on the ground, usually from ricochets. Sometimes, German aircraft flying at low level would machine gun villages as they flew over.

There was a general assumption on the ground that those who bailed out were enemy pilots. We have seen what happened to Nicholson VC, and it was not uncommon for RAF pilots to be subjected to searching questioning by the Home Guard or local policeman before their *bona fides* were established in the eyes of those who had 'captured' them. For the Czechs, Poles, French and Belgians, whose command of the English language was often sketchy, it was even more difficult.

The Home Guard and others in uniform spent much time in guarding crashed aircraft against people wanting to take bits as souvenirs. Downed RAF fighters were recovered and, if possible, repaired or else cannibalised and used for spare parts. German aircraft were, of course, an invaluable source of technical intelligence and had to be carefully inspected by experts before being taken to aircraft 'graveyards'. Sometimes, too, useful documents might be found on them, which could help maintain an accurate Luftwaffe order of battle and give an indication of future intentions.

Much excitement could be generated in hunting for downed German aircrew. The country writer A G Street was a member of the Home Guard in Wiltshire and recalled such a hunt, a success-

ful one. 'As I was driving home I realised that I, civilian, had just experienced my first taste of war, and that I disliked it intensely. I was dead keen to hunt that fellow, felt the same exhilaration as I did when the hounds were running, and would have shot him on the instant if need be. But, somehow, when he was caught I had no further quarrel with him.' There are, in fact, no recorded incidents of German airmen resisting capture or of any being shot on the ground. A few, though, were roughly handled by irate civilians and had to be rescued by servicemen. Many, however, displayed arrogance, much of it brought about by the certain knowledge that they would not remain prisoners for very long. Operation SEALION would see to that.

In themselves these prisoners could be a useful and sometimes invaluable source of intelligence. Trained interrogators were based at RAF airfields and other service establishments. They would be notified as soon as an enemy aircraft crashed in their area. They would then inspect the aircraft and visit the prisoner, who would

Above left: *Waiting for the next sortie.*

Above: *Pilot Officer Stevens of 17 Squadron with his fitter and rigger.*

Below left: *Kenley under attack, 18 August 1940.*

Below right: *An unexploded bomb, which landed on the parade ground at RAF Hemswell, is detonated.*

often initially be housed in the local police station, in order to carry out the first interrogation. This was concerned with establishing the prisoner's unit and base, details of how he was shot down, and his knowledge, if any, of future plans. In cases where the interrogator suspected that the airman might have additional information he would refer him for detailed interrogation.

This took place at the Combined Services Detailed Interrogation Centre at Trent Park, Cockfosters, in north London. Here all sorts of techniques were used, including bugged rooms and stool pigeons. A vast file index system was built up with details of individual Luftwaffe personnel. This could often be used to good effect to convince the prisoner that his captors knew all about him already and that there was little point in withholding any information. It is interesting to note that the Luftwaffe used almost exactly the same techniques when dealing with Allied aircrew.

If Fighter Command was becoming tired then so was the Luftwaffe. Their losses during the period 24 August – 6 September were also high, 545 aircraft from all causes. None of their *Staffeln* had been rotated. Many, especially the Me109 pilots, were flying two sorties a day and each meant a double crossing of the Channel. It was this rather than combat *per se* that preyed on their minds for they knew that, in spite of their good air-sea rescue service, no one could survive long if forced to ditch in the sea. It was something they called 'Channel sickness'. Yet, their morale was perhaps higher than it had been earlier in the battle, when they had experienced the realisation that it was going to be no walk-over. They calculated that the RAF was now reduced to 600 fighters, of which 420 were operational, and a reserve of 100, with production running at 300 fighters per month. In their turn, *Luftflotten 2* and *3* still had 1158 bombers (772 operational), 232 Me110s (129 operational), and 787 Me109s (623 operational). Their superiority in numbers was therefore still overwhelming and they believed RAF Fighter Command to be 'severely crippled'. It was thus a question of 'one more heave' and the job would be done.

Below: *601 Squadron Hurricanes refuel and rearm while the pilots, including Lord Beaverbrook's son Max Aitken (left of picture), anxiously stand by.*

Above: 66 *Squadron Spitfires scramble at Coltishall.*

CHAPTER V

THE CLIMAX

Dornier 17s over London's East End, 7 September 1940.

RAF Bomber Command's attacks on Berlin had resulted in Hitler informing Goering that he could now turn his attention to London. On 3 September Wilhelm Keitel, Chief of Staff of the German Armed Forces issued an order postponing the mounting of SEALION from 15 to 21 September, with a final decision being made ten days before. Clearly this would be largely dependent on the Luftwaffe's success in the meantime. On that same day, the 3rd, Goering conferred with Kesselring and Sperrle at The Hague to inform them of his intention to switch to London as the main objective. Sperrle was not in favour of this since he believed that the defences had not yet been sufficiently degraded. Kesselring, however, welcomed the prospect. His Me109 pilots had become increasingly frustrated in their seeming inability to tempt sufficient numbers of RAF fighters into the air at once to make a worthwhile target. Furthermore, even if the Luftwaffe did manage to destroy the 11 Group airfields the RAF could still use airfields further north and these would be beyond the range of the Me109s. The Germans, too, could point to Warsaw and Rotterdam as examples of air attacks bringing about capitulations. An offensive against London would make the British people less prepared to resist invasion. The die was thus cast.

The weather on the morning of 7 September was fine, as it had been for the past eight days. It did not bring the usual blips, which heralded yet another Luftwaffe attack, on the Chain Home radar screens. Indeed, the only activity was the successful interception of a Do215 reconnaissance aircraft by Spitfires of 266 Squadron based at Wittering. The previous day had been a hard one, with the 11 Group airfields taking yet another hammering, together with attacks on Shorts of Rochester and the Hurricane factory at Weybridge. The oil storage tanks at Thameshaven, which had become a

Left: *The Luftwaffe turns to night attacks on London – St Paul's Cathedral stands defiant.*

Right: *Thames fire tenders fighting fires in the London docks.*

Below left: *Personal protection from the Luftwaffe's bombs.*

Bottom left: *A bombed out East End family keeps cheerful in a communal shelter.*

new attraction for the Luftwaffe during the past few days, had also been hit once more and the fires acted as a beacon for the night bombers. Of growing concern was the concentration of barges in Belgian and Dutch ports, which caused the Chiefs of Staff to issue a warning that invasion was likely within the next three days. The pause on the morning of 7 September was therefore seen as the lull before the storm, but for all that a welcome one for all those involved in the battle.

On the other side of the Channel, however, there was frenetic activity on the *Luftflotte 2* airfields. Three hundred bombers and 600 fighters were being prepared for the onslaught on London. Goering himself had decided to take personal charge and was now at St Omer with Kesselring to watch the armada set out across the Channel.

Just after 1530 hours a blip appeared on the screen of the CHL station at Foreness on the east coast of Kent. Then the CH station at Dover reported twenty plus bandits over the Pas de Calais. The size of the raid grew with each report. Eleven 11 Group squadrons were scrambled, and were shortly afterwards joined by Bader's Duxford Wing and other 12 Group squadrons. The controllers, however, were having problems. The plots did not merely show one large concentration, but a collection of formations, which seemed to join up and split again apparently at random. Hence it was difficult to give precise directions to the fighters aloft as to where to look. All they could do was to assume that the 11 Group airfields were the target once again and to keep the fighters orbiting above them. Then the sighting reports from the air began to come in. The separate groups of Heinkels, Junkers, Dorniers and their attendant fighters had now begun to come together. One RAF pilot recalled that 'as far as you could see, there was nothing but German aircraft coming in, wave after wave'. Another called it 'a breathtaking sight'.

It was only then that the penny dropped. The raiders were not after the airfields, but London itself. It was too late. As the first Hurricanes cut into the bombers and their escort, bombs began to fall on the Woolwich arsenal in south-east London. The anti-aircraft gun barrage opened up, but did not bother the bombers much. As each successive wave arrived, the area under attack increased, to take in the docks and London's East End. An Air Raid Precautions (ARP) warden: 'The miniature silver planes circling round and round the target area in such perfect formation that they looked like a children's toy model of flying boats or chair-o-planes at a fair.' The bombs came down 'with a tearing sound as well as a whistle; they did not fall, they rushed at enormous velocity, as though dragged down towards the earth by some supernaturally gigantic magnet'. One of the volunteer fire watchers standing on St Paul's Cathedral commented: 'It is the end of the world.'

Soon London's streets were filled with the shrill clang of fire engine and ambulance bells. Above, as each wave unloaded its bombs it turned away north and then eastwards and out over the North Sea. By this stage they had lost their escorting Me109s, who, now low on fuel, were streaking south on the most direct course for home. Later waves were now being engaged by the 11 Group squadrons, but their Me109s had the better of it, 249 Squadron alone losing half its strength of Hurricanes by the end of the day. The Duxford Wing, making its debut, had a frustrating time. Only Bader's squadron made contact with the raiders, but they were 5000 feet above the Hurricanes when first spotted. Nevertheless, Bader was able to reach them in time and he and his pilots claimed eleven shot down at a cost of one Hurricane shot down and its pilot killed, another Hurricane crash-landed and Bader's own aircraft damaged. In all, by the time the last wave of bombers had crossed back over the coast 36 had been destroyed, but it had cost 28 Spitfires and Hurricanes to achieve this. It had been the Luftwaffe's day and Goering could be well pleased with his fighters.

Park had happened to be visiting Dowding and the two had watched the attack on the Bentley Priory plotting board. Flying over London that evening Park saw the flames and smoke of several fires. It made him very angry, but 'I said "Thank God", because I realised that the methodical Germans had at last switched their attacks away from my vital airfields'. The Chiefs of Staff, having talked with Churchill in Downing Street, took a grimmer view. They concluded that the invasion was now about to take place. Shortly after 2000 hours they issued the codeword CROMWELL. This was passed rapidly down the chain of command and units deployed to their battle positions. One or two local commanders, taking the codeword to mean that the invasion had already begun, ordered the local church bells to be rung. In one or two cases bridges were even demolished.

The Luftwaffe's day was not, however, yet done. Shortly after CROMWELL was issued Sperrle's night bombers began to appear. Although darkness had not yet fallen, for some inexplicable reason only two Hurricanes were scrambled, but they merely covered their base at Tangmere. Later Blenheim night fighters were scrambled, but were troubled by continuous anti-aircraft fire and

searchlights, and had no success. Between 2100 and 0300 hours the capital was under continuous attack. Fires were triggered in many parts by the numerous incendiaries dropped with the HE bombs. Three main line railway stations were put totally out of action and many roads were blocked. Four hundred and thirty civilians lost their lives, a further thousand were seriously injured and many were made homeless. Just one German bomber failed to return.

Yet, the British were not totally passive that night. RAF Bomber Command sent up 92 aircraft. Some went to the Ruhr, others to drop incendiaries on German forests in an effort to start fires, but

Above: *He111 nose gunner covers another Heinkel.*

Left: *Bombing up a Ju88. The Ju88 entered Luftwaffe service in 1939 and remained in production to the end of the war.*

Below: *Me109 repair shop. The Me109 too served throughout the war.*

Top left: *Air battle over Big Ben.*

Above left: *Bomb crater. The corrugated iron is the remains of an Anderson air raid shelter, named after the Home Secretary. The occupants of the shelter evidently survived this very near miss.*

the bulk to attack invasion barges. They would continue to pound these over the next few nights, but would also attack German North Sea and Baltic ports and, on the night of 10/11 September, the Potsdamer station in Berlin.

Early morning RAF reconnaissance flights on the 8th revealed no indication that the invasion fleet was putting to sea, and there was little air activity during the day. The Luftwaffe needed a pause after its 'maximum effort' of the previous 24 hours. This gave Dowding the opportunity to introduce a scheme designed to relieve some of the pressure on his battered squadrons. They were now to be categorised into three types. Category A were those which were operationally fit and would be deployed with 11 Group. Category B were partially fit, with a number of experienced pilots, but still needing time to bring them up to Category A. They would be deployed in 10 and 12 Groups. Finally, the unfit Category C squadrons, with few experienced pilots, would be posted to 13 Group. In order for the scheme to work, however, Dowding was forced to adopt a measure that he had so far resisted once the battle had started. Squadron esprit de corps was a vital commodity and much of it came from keeping the same pilots together. Now, in the interests of spreading experience throughout his command, he began cross-posting experienced pilots between squadrons.

While Londoners tried to clear up the wreckage, Churchill visited the badly hit East End, the poorest area of the city. He inspected an air raid shelter in which forty people had been killed the previous night. The Eastenders were delighted to see him: 'We can take it. Give it 'em back.'

That night, though, the bombers came again. Damage was again widespread and another 400 people were killed. Again, it was the East End which got the worst of it. Next day, a secret Home Intelligence Report noted that 'in dockside areas the population is showing visible signs of its nerve cracking from constant ordeals.' And yet, these were just the first nights of a winter's worth of attacks on London.

On 9 September the Luftwaffe made another daylight attack on London. This time they did not get through and lost 28 aircraft. RAF losses were nineteen. There was damage to the suburbs, however, caused by hastily jettisoned bombs, an indication of the savagery of the 11 and 12 Group attacks. On that day *Luftflotten 2* and *3* received new instructions. Kesselring was to concentrate on key military and commercial targets in the London area by day, while Sperrle would take on government buildings and the docks by night. Interestingly, the British Combined Intelligence Committee soon noted that 'the selection of targets for attack was evidence of a thorough and carefully thought-out plan. There is insufficient evidence, however, to show whether it was designed for its nuisance value by the disruption of passenger traffic and of the transit of goods for industrial purposes, or whether it was definitely intended as a prelude to invasion' – an oblique compliment to the accuracy of the Luftwaffe's bombing.

That night the inhabitants of London were able to get a full night's sleep as Sperrle's bombers left them alone. Cloud and rain on the 10th prevented major operations by day, but Sperrle was back that night, not only over London, but Merseyside and South Wales as well. Hitler was pleased with the way in which the assault on London was going and was beginning to hope that SEALION could be mounted merely to follow up the decisive victory which the Luftwaffe was about to gain. He now ordered that the invasion should take place on 24 September, but that he would make a final decision on the 14th.

Better weather on the 11th meant another daylight attack. This was a much more determined and carefully thought out attack than that of the 9th. Firstly, a number of feints were made to get 11 Group's fighters aloft. Then, at about 1520 hours, the Dover CH station identified two groups of aircraft, one of over fifty and the other of over one hundred aircraft. Significantly they were flying very much higher than previously, at a height of 24,000ft as compared to the more normal 16-20,000ft. Once again the fighter escort was large and they kept the RAF fighters at bay as the streams flew over Kent towards London. Not only did the Me109s do this, but also by the end of the day had actually shot down more fighters than *Luftflotte 2*'s total losses – 29 to 25. Indeed, it was only

Left: *Luftwaffe ace Helmuth Wick and* (above) *his Me109E. Note the victory markings on the tail of the aircraft.*

Left: *He111 pilot and bomb aimer.*

Below: *Nose gunner's view of a Ju88 formation.*

Bottom: *Goering (centre) sees for himself. Inspecting a Stuka with Erhard Milch (right).*

after the bombers had dropped their loads and the Me109s had turned for home that the Hurricanes and Spitfires were able to claim some success. Bader's wing succeeded in getting all three squadrons in among the bombers and claimed twenty shot down for the loss of four Hurricanes and two pilots.

Among the bombs that did fall were some that were counter-productive for the Luftwaffe. One bomber flew up Pall Mall and dropped bombs on Buckingham Palace, causing slight damage. The Royal Family was in residence at the time, and the Queen commented: 'Now we can look the people of the East End in the face.' It was a remark made more pertinent by the fact that she and the King had visited the Eastenders two days before.

That night the bombers were over London once more, as they would be most nights until the official end of the battle. A large time bomb fell close to St Paul's Cathedral. The task of defusing unexploded bombs was that of the Bomb Disposal Section of the Royal Engineers. It was a job that required the highest technical skills and cold blooded courage. In this case, the bomb was recovered and driven at high speed to Hackney Marshes, where it was safely exploded. In recognition of the great gallantry being shown by servicemen and civilians in the face of the bombing, King George VI announced, on 23 September, that he had created a new award for courage, the George Cross, which was to rank next to the Victoria Cross. He also instituted a lesser award, the George Medal. Two of the first recipients of the George Cross were Lieutenant Robert Davies and Sapper Wylie who had dealt with the St Paul's bomb.

By now many Londoners had decided that the safest place to be at night was the Underground. Initially the authorities had tried to prevent this, but had to give in to popular pressure. As night fell, more and more people took their bedding and settled in the stations for the night.

Cloud during the next two days restricted the Luftwaffe's daylight operations, although single aircraft took advantage of it to penetrate as far north as Yorkshire to attack railways, factories, and

military installations. On the 14th the weather was marginal and Kesselring sent a small force of bombers, which attacked the London suburbs, killing some fifty people, and the seaside resorts of Eastbourne and Brighton. Fourteen aircraft on each side were

Left: *A. G. Lewis, a South African pilot serving with 85 Squadron during the Battle. Lewis shot down six German aircraft in one day during September 1940.*

Above: *Cutaway drawing of a Hurricane I in 85 Squadron markings.*

shot down. On this day Hitler postponed the invasion until 27 September, setting the next decision day as the 17th. The Luftwaffe had achieved excellent results and there was a very real opportunity of forcing Britain to her knees. Another four or five days of good weather were, however, needed to achieve the complete elimination of RAF Fighter Command and total victory. He also believed that the air campaign and British uncertainty as to when the invasion was going to take place were having a significant psychological effect on the country and a state of mass hysteria could be created.

Above: *Hurricane I in flight.*

On the morning of Sunday, 15 September Churchill decided to visit the Headquarters of 11 Group at Uxbridge in Middlesex. Before dawn the Luftwaffe had sent out aircraft to check on the weather, which was guaranteed fine and perfect for a *Luftflotte 2* maximum effort. By 1100 hours the Chain Home stations were detecting a massive build-up over the Pas de Calais. Half an hour later the air raid sirens around London began their dismal wail as more and more squadrons were scrambled. This time the Fighter Command controllers had had sufficient time to get their aircraft up to an advantageous height before the bombers and their escorts arrived. Significantly, too, Kesselring did not employ his normal feints, a sign of his over-confidence. No less than 22 squadrons from Nos 10, 11, and 12 Groups were scrambled, a larger number than on any previous day of the battle. They began to harry the bombers almost as soon as they crossed the English coast. A squadron commander takes up the story:

'As we were climbing in a southerly direction at 15,000 feet we saw thirty Heinkels supported by fifty Me109s 4,000 feet above them, and twenty Me110s to a flank, approaching us from above. We turned and climbed, flying in the same direction as the bombers with the whole squadron stringed out in echelon to port up sun, so that each man had a view of the enemy.

"A" flight timed their attack to perfection, coming down sun in a power dive on the enemy's left flank. As each was selecting his

Right: *Ju88s. Comparatively few Ju88s served in the Battle of Britain but the design later proved to be versatile and successful.*

Below: *Do17, known as the 'flying pencil'.*

Opposite, above: *Hitler meets Mussolini, but initially turns down his offer to send Italian aircraft to participate in the Luftwaffe's defeat of Britain.*

Opposite, below: *Luftwaffe armourer prepares to reload an aircraft's machine guns.*

own man, the Me110 escort roared in to intercept with cannons blazing at 1,000 yards range, but they were two seconds too late – too late to engage our fighters, but just in time to make them hesitate long enough to miss the bomber leader. Two Heinkels heeled out of the formation.

Meanwhile, the Me110s had flashed out of sight, leaving the way clear for "B" flight, as long as the Me109s stayed above. "B" flight leader knew how to bide his time, but just as he was about to launch his attack the Heinkels did the unbelievable thing. They turned south; into the sun; and into him. With his first burst the leader destroyed the leading bomber, which blew up with such force that it knocked a wing off the left-hand bomber. A little bank and a burst from his guns sent the right-hand Heinkel out of the formation with smoke pouring out of both engines. Before returning home he knocked out an Me109. Four aircraft destroyed for an expenditure of 1,200 rounds . . .'

In spite of the success of these attacks the bombers did reach London. Most bombs fell south of the River Thames, but one stick caught Buckingham Palace again, destroying the Queen's private apartments and leaving an unexploded bomb on the lawn. Their Majesties were not, however, at home. As the Me109s turned away, leaving the bombers on their own, the No 12 Group squadrons arrived on the scene, including the Duxford Wing, which had been swollen to five squadrons. Bader's pilots later claimed to have shot down 26 aircraft. The fighting continued until the bombers were way back over the coast.

As had so often been the case during the past weeks, this attack was merely an appetiser. Just after lunch, taken by Dowding's pilots as a hasty sandwich and mug of tea close to their aircraft, the plots began to appear once more. This time it was a much larger force, up to 200 bombers in all in three waves. They were much quicker in forming up and were across the coast before the 11 Group squadrons had gained sufficient height. There was, however, compensation for this in that the formations seemed to halt over the Sevenoaks area and mill around, probably because of lack of coordination over the rendezvous with their Me109 escorts. The main battle itself was fought over the southern part of London. As in the morning, it was just as the Me109s turned for home that the 10 and 12 Group squadrons arrived. What the fighter pilots noticed was that the bombers were now hesitant about driving home their attacks. Many merely jettisoned their bombs and in one case a Hurricane pilot reported that a formation of eight Dorniers just scattered in the face of his lone aircraft. There was a sense that the RAF had now achieved moral superiority over their opponents, an indication that the Luftwaffe's fortunes were on the ebb.

On the ground it was not so immediately obvious what had happened. At the height of the action Churchill, watching it in the No 11 Group operations room, turned to Park and asked him what reserves he had left. 'None' was the answer. It was only after two smaller raids by *Luftflotte 3* on Portland and Southampton had been successfully parried in the early evening and the claims from the squadrons had been totted up that the magnitude of what had happened became clear. It seemed that the Luftwaffe had lost no less than 185 aircraft, as against less than 40 RAF fighters. In truth this figure was vastly exaggerated and the true totals were 60 Luftwaffe and 26 RAF. Even so, the British were right to herald this day as a great victory, one that henceforth would be known as Battle of Britain Day.

The Luftwaffe report on the day admitted that it had been 'unusually disadvantageous', especially in the number of bombers which had been lost. Once again Goering, in his frustration and disappointment, turned on his fighter pilots, blaming them for

Issued by the Ministry of Information in co-operation with the War Office and the Ministry of Home Security

Beating the INVADER

A MESSAGE FROM THE PRIME MINISTER

IF invasion comes, everyone—young or old, men and women—will be eager to play their part worthily. By far the greater part of the country will not be immediately involved. Even along our coasts, the greater part will remain unaffected. But where the enemy lands, or tries to land, there will be most violent fighting. Not only will there be the battles when the enemy tries to come ashore, but afterwards there will fall upon his lodgments very heavy British counter-attacks, and all the time the lodgments will be under the heaviest attack by British bombers. The fewer civilians or non-combatants in these areas, the better—apart from essential workers who must remain. So if you are advised by the authorities to leave the place where you live, it is your duty to go elsewhere when you are told to leave When the attack begins, it will be too late to go ; and, unless you receive definite instructions to move, your duty then will be to stay where you are. You will have to get into the safest place you can find, and stay there until the battle is over. For all of you then the order and the duty will be : " STAND FIRM ".

This also applies to people inland if any considerable number of parachutists or air-borne troops are landed in their neighbourhood. Above all, they must not cumber the roads. Like their fellow-countrymen on the coasts, they must " STAND FIRM ". The Home Guard, supported by strong mobile columns wherever the enemy's numbers require it, will immediately come to grips with the invaders, and there is little doubt will soon destroy them.

Throughout the rest of the country where there is no fighting going on and no close cannon fire or rifle fire can be heard, everyone will govern his conduct by the second great order and duty, namely, " CARRY ON ". It may easily be some weeks before the invader has been totally destroyed, that is to say, killed or captured to the last man who has landed on our shores. Meanwhile, all work must be continued to the utmost, and no time lost.

The following notes have been prepared to tell everyone in rather more detail what to do, and they should be carefully studied. Each man and woman should think out a clear plan of personal action in accordance with the general scheme.

Winston S. Churchill

STAND FIRM

1. What do I do if fighting breaks out in my neighbourhood?

Keep indoors or in your shelter until the battle is over. If you can have a trench ready in your garden or field, so much the better. You may want to use it for protection if your house is damaged. But if you are at work, or if you have special orders, carry on as long as possible and only take cover when danger approaches. If you are on your way to work, finish your journey if you can.

If you see an enemy tank, or a few enemy soldiers, do not assume that the enemy are in control of the area. What you have seen may be a party sent on in advance, or stragglers from the main body who can easily be rounded up.

Above: *A 72 Squadron Spitfire.*

Left: *What to do if the Germans do invade.*

Above right: *'Contact!' The flames from the exhaust are normal as the engine on this Spitfire fires.*

Bottom right; *Winston Churchill addressing Parliament's own Home Guard detachment.*

their failure to prevent the RAF from getting in amongst the bombers. He refused to recognise that the root cause of the problem was the limited range of the Me109. Two days later Hitler postponed SEALION until further notice. 'We have conquered France at the cost of 30,000 men. During one night of crossing the Channel we could lose many times that – and success is not certain.'

Nevertheless, 15 September did not mark the end of the battle. Goering was still determined to wear down the British fighter strength and the Blitz on London and other cities was to continue. All he still needed was another spell of fine weather. The next two days did not grant him this and air activity by day was slight, although the night attacks continued. In the meantime, Bomber Command had been continuing its offensive on the barges. On the night of 17/18 September no less than 194 aircraft were dispatched, the highest total so far during the war, two thirds of them against the Channel ports. No less than 85 barges were destroyed at Dunkirk alone. As a result, on the 19th the German High Command ordered a thinning out of invasion barges. This was picked up by photographic air reconnaissance and on the 22nd CROMWELL, which had remained in force for the past two weeks, was cancelled.

On 21 September, the Lord Mayor of London, Sir William Coxen made a broadcast to New York. 'Today London stands as the very bulwark of civilisation and freedom. These streets of my city will be defended to the last. London City has sometimes been attacked, but never sacked. London has steeled herself for resistance and victory . . .' In reply, Mayor Fiorello La Guardia of New York, said: 'Bravo, London. We have listened to you with fascinated admiration. We are praying for you. Thumbs up, London.'

At the end of June 1940 few Americans gave Britain any chance of surviving more than a few weeks. No one was stronger in this belief than Joseph Kennedy, the US ambassador to London and father of a future President of the United States, who told President Roosevelt that Britain had nothing left but her courage, and that this was of little consequence. He did his best to frustrate US citizens who wanted to join Britain's armed forces and sent back

Above: *Ju88 with an Me109 escort.*

Right: *HM King George VI talking to Al Deere while visiting some of 'The Few.'*

Opposite, above: *Girls of the Auxiliary Territorial Service (ATS) operating a rangefinder in support of an anti-aircraft gun battery.*

Opposite, below: *Luftwaffe aircrew during a 'ditching' drill.*

ever more pessimistic reports to Washington. It was, however, the American journalists in London who told their people of the British will to resist and the way in which they were doing it. Most notable was Ed Murrow of the Columbia Broadcasting Service (CBS), whose broadcasts were to become one of the hallmarks of the Blitz. Their reports did much slowly to turn the USA from its deeply embedded isolationism.

During the ten days after 15 September there was a reduction in Luftwaffe activity. It now mainly consisted of fighter sweeps and attacks on aircraft factories, which were more successful than hitherto. On the 24th an attack on the Spitfire factory at Woolston caused 150 casualties among the staff. Next day it was the turn of the Bristol works at Filton. The controllers were caught by surprise, believing from their course that the target was the Westland factory at Yeovil. A last minute change of direction caught the RAF

Left: *Recovering an Me109E of JG27 from Windsor Great Park, where it had crashed after stalling while executing a sharp turn in order to attack two Avro Anson trainers.*

Right: *London must have looked very defenceless to this He111 crew.*

Below left: *Luftwaffe aircrew preparing for their next attack on England.*

Below right: *ATS girls in AA Command did everything apart from actually pull the trigger. Here they are operating a kine-Theodolite. This photographed shell bursts in order to make the predictor, which governed gun laying, more accurate.*

fighters off balance and, although five bombers were shot down on the way, considerable damage was caused to the Filton factory, with 250 of its work force killed or injured. Further extensive damage was done to the Woolston factory on the 26th. This encouraged the *Luftwaffe* to make larger daylight attacks on the following day. *Luftflotte 2* dispatched 55 Ju88s to London and *Luftflotte 3* thirty Heinkels to Bristol. It was a disaster, with most of the bombers never reaching their targets. Fifty-seven were shot down, although the contemporary Air Ministry claim was 133, at a cost of 28 RAF fighters. For the next two days, during which the weather remained fine, small groups of bombers with large escorts appeared over southern England. They made little impression, and aircraft casualties on both sides were about the same.

On the last day of the month came the largest daylight raids since the 15th. Activity over the Kent coast began at 0800 hours, with groups of German fighters doing their 'coat trailing' act. Park refused to be drawn and awaited the bombers, which appeared an hour later. They were composed of two *Gruppen* of Ju88s. For once they appeared over the coast near Dungeness unescorted; another case of confusion over the rendezvous. No 11 Group sent up some 150 fighters to tackle them. They shot down a number before the Me109s finally arrived on the scene. By then the bombers had had enough and were jettisoning their bombs before turning for home. Then, at midday, *Luftflotte 3* sent two formations to attack Bristol and the Westland works at Yeovil. Five 10 Group squadrons were sent up to deal with the Heinkels flying to Yeovil. They prevented them from reaching their target, the Sherborne area receiving most of their bombs. An aircraft factory north of Bristol was the target of the second prong of Sperrle's attack and it was carried out by nineteen Me110s from *Eroberungsgruppe 210*. Although they pressed home their attack with the utmost gallantry, they lost four aircraft, including that of their commander.

The day operations of 30 September cost Kesselring and Sperrle 48 aircraft as against 20 RAF fighters. It was another costly reverse. Indeed, during the month no less than four *Geschwader* commanders, thirteen *Gruppe* and 28 *Staffel* leaders had been lost, and one *Kampfgeschwader* had suffered 30 per cent aircraft casualties, with 160 aircrew lost. The message was clear. The massed daylight attacks had not worked and never again would they be employed over England. It was the end of the penultimate phase of the battle.

CHAPTER VI

THE LAST PHASE

A London railway terminus (St Pancras) is hit. It is remarkable how quickly the damage was repaired.

While the battle by day can be viewed as having been won by the end of September in that the Luftwaffe had failed to achieve the necessary preconditions for invasion, this did not mean that the problems faced by Britain in the air were at an end. The night raids continued unabated throughout October. London itself was attacked every night except one during the month and by a force averaging 150 bombers. Unlike by day, there was little to stop them from doing so.

All the resources that RAF Fighter Command had to combat the night bombers were its two squadrons of Defiants and six of Blenheims. In order to address the problem a high-powered committee, the Night Air Defence Committee, had been set up in mid-September and had recommended that Hurricanes and Spitfires be employed as well. This Dowding opposed for the practical reason that their cockpits were simply not large enough to install airborne radar. The Air Council insisted, however, that he earmark three Hurricane squadrons to this task, which he did most unwillingly. They could hardly be expected to make much positive contribution, while the other two types were generally too slow, even if they did have the then still-primitive first-generation airborne radar. Consequently, the night bomber always got through at this time and would continue to do so until the twin-engined Bristol Beaufighter equipped with the Mark IV AI radar appeared early in 1941. Unless the Aspirins could confuse the *Knickebein* equipped bombers, Londoners and others just had to grin and bear the Blitz.

But operations by day also witnessed problems, albeit new ones, during October. Goering was still insistent that Britain continue

to be attacked by day as well as by night. Since conventional mass bomber attacks by day had failed to work, new tactics needed to be employed. The answer lay in the fighter-bomber, or *Jagdbombern*, but more commonly called Jabos by the Luftwaffe, the bomb carrying Me109s and Me110s, which *Eroberungsgruppe 210* had been using with fair success. Instead, however, of sending them against England at low level they would fly at high altitude, 25-32,000 feet. The defenders would only have a maximum of 20 minutes warning time and it was well nigh impossible for the RAF's fighters to reach these heights in time to intercept the Jabos en route to their targets. Also such heights were near the Hurricane's service ceiling.

Left: *An He111 is prepared for another attack on England. Presumably a posed photograph, since it is unlikely that the engines would have been running while bombs were being loaded.*

Below left: *A German air reconnaissance photograph of burning oil storage tanks at Newhaven on the Thames. Oil was an important target and, if denied it, Britain would have been unable to continue the fight.*

Right: *A Luftwaffe recruiting poster. Goering was to enlarge the Luftwaffe to such an extent that it would include ground formations which fought with the Army.*

These Jabo attacks, sometimes with a few Ju88s accompanying them, began on 1 October and continued almost every day during the month. As many as 1000 Me109 sorties, including many by the conventional fighter version, which flew escort to the Jabos, per day were not unusual. No 11 Group's Spitfire squadrons were put under pressures more intense than at any time during the battle. They found themselves scrambling as many as four times a day and pilots became so exhausted that as soon as they landed they fell asleep. Park did his best, but on 8 October was forced to adopt the old pre-radar tactic of standing patrols, which was wasteful of resources and increased pilot fatigue even more.

By this time, the 'old lags' who had survived the summer and early autumn fighting were increasingly succumbing to combat fatigue. At least now the pilot shortage was not what it had been in September, but every squadron still wanted to maintain a fair number of veterans. Not only were those the ones that shot down the enemy aircraft, but also it was through them that the novices learned their trade. To keep them combat flying for too long, however, was to sign their death warrants. Their tempers grew short, their nicotine and alcohol intake increased, but, more serious, their reactions grew sluggish. When this happened, they became easy meat for the Me109s. They had, therefore, to be posted. Their

Right: *A Hurricane's Merlin engine exposed.*

Opposite left: *Flight Sergeant (later Wing Commander) Donald Kingaby DFM and two bars.*

Opposite right: *Flight Lieutenant Stan Turner DFC, one of the Canadians in Bader's 242 Squadron.*

Below: *Hurricanes of 501 Squadron.*

SD

opposite numbers in the Luftwaffe were by now suffering in the same way, and also had to endure the Channel Sickness as well. Yet, the Luftwaffe did not adopt the same rest system as the RAF. Their pilots just flew on and on.

Another breed of casualty were the burns cases. The Battle of Britain marked a milestone in the history of plastic surgery. There are still aircrew alive today, both RAF and Luftwaffe, who owe much to a man called Archibald McIndoe. He was a plastic surgeon who ran the Maxillo-Facial Unit at the Queen Victoria Hospital, East Grinstead. Those who were burned when their aircraft were shot up normally suffered most to the face and hands and it was to East Grinstead that they were brought. McIndoe developed the concept of grafting skin from other parts of the body to rebuild hands and, especially faces. The results may not have been aesthetically perfect, but his secret was his ability to get his burns cases to live with their altered appearances and to continue to hold their heads high. It was Richard Hillary DFC, the epitome of the 'long haired boys' of the RAFVR, who first brought McIndoe's great achievements to the attention of the public in his classic book *The Last Enemy*. Dreadfully burned during the battle, under McIndoe's ministrations he recovered to fly on fighter operations again, only to be killed in action in 1942. Ever afterwards the patients called themselves, with great pride, 'McIndoe's guinea pigs' and designed a special tie to reflect this. Later he was knighted for his services.

During the first week of October the Jabos and Ju88s attacked a number of targets, mainly aircraft factories and airfields. Because the tonnage of bombs which the Jabos could carry was only a fraction of that of the bombers the damage was much less. Nevertheless, they did have their successes. On the 3rd a single Ju88 managed to get through to the de Havilland aircraft factory at Hatfield

Above right: *Londoners take to the Underground to escape the Blitz.*

Right: *One way of keeping up morale in the Underground shelters.*

Opposite, top: *Me109 shot down in Sussex, 25 October 1940.*

Opposite, left: *H M Stephen (left) and J C Mungo-Park of 74 Squadron.*

Opposite, right: *An Me109 arrives in the USA for public exhibition, one of the many ways of helping to persuade Americans that they must enter the war.*

in Hertfordshire and successfully bombed it. Two days later Southampton suffered once more, the defence having been caught wrong-footed. This day saw the highest number of Fighter Command sorties in the battle, no less than 1175. Me110s struck at West Malling airfield, now finally completed, but suffered at the hands of 303 (Polish) Squadron, losing four shot down and two crashlanding in France. The Luftwaffe had better success against 607 Squadron, who lost four of their Spitfires. Yet, Fighter Command's record number of sorties only achieved 13 victories at a cost of eight British fighters and illustrates only too clearly the frustrations of this last phase of the battle.

The autumnal weather also began to create problems of its own. Fog became almost a daily occurrence and made flying very much more difficult. The rate of flying accidents on both sides rose sharply. The worst on the British side was on 18 October when four Polish pilots killed themselves while attempting to force land on Sandown racecourse in Surrey. Low cloud, though, assisted the Luftwaffe, enabling bombers, often single ones, to get through and attack 11 Group airfields, causing some damage and casualties to personnel.

On 8 October a German communique, referring to an attack on London the previous night,stated that it had 'brought the succession of reprisal attacks which have shaken Britain on a culminating point.' That same morning low-flying aircraft beat up some of the main thoroughfares in the capital, hitting trams and trains and knocking out a bus. The 12th signalled London's 200th alert, and the 14th and 15th also marked the heaviest raids yet on London by night. On the second occasion over 400 bombers took part. RAF Bomber Command was doing its best to strike back, but seldom could mount more than 150 sorties by night and the range of targets it had to attack meant that its raids were little more than pinpricks. It continued to harrass the Channel ports, but was also attacking factories, oil, communications and the German shipbuilding industry.

On 17 October a meeting was held in the Air Ministry, its subject 'Major Day Tactics in the Fighter Force'. It was chaired by Sholto Douglas, Deputy Chief of the Air Staff, and among those who attended were Dowding, Brand, Leigh-Mallory, Park and Bader, by far the most junior member present. The purpose was to resolve the Big Wing question for once and for all. Douglas recalled that there was a heated argument between Park and Leigh-Mallory, but it seems that Dowding said little. The general conclusion was that employment of big wings, provided they had sufficient warning, had great advantages, although it was not necessarily the total answer. Dowding also agreed to allow 12 Group wings to 'participate freely in suitable operations' in Park's area and that he would resolve any command and control problems. When Dowding, Park and Brand received their copies of the minutes they protested. Park, especially did not feel that his case had been properly reflected and pointed to the problems of Bader's wing coming into his area without warning and creating confusion in the control organisation. The Air Ministry, however, declined to amend the minutes. This debate was to produce an unfortunate aftertaste.

The battle rumbled on amid worsening weather conditions. On 26 October, after night raids on London and Harwich, a German communique announced that some 200 Italian aircraft had taken part. Mussolini had offered, in July, to participate in SEALION, but Hitler had politely declined this. Now increasingly angered by RAF Bomber Command's occasional attacks on northern Italy, he managed to persuade the Germans to allow a contingent from the *Regia Aeronautica* to take part in attacks on England. This night operation was their first appearance, but they would operate on two occasions by day.

The first of these was on 29 October, which marked the last day of heavy fighting during the battle. For once the weather was reasonable, with sunlight appearing through the autumn haze. At about 1030 hours bandits were identified over the Pas de Calais. They turned out to be an Me109 *Gruppe*, which crossed the coast

Left: *The remains of an Italian bomber shot down during a raid on Harwich, 11 November 1940, the second and last Italian appearance over England.*

Below left: *End of mission – a Hurricane section coming into land. According to the original official caption this picture was taken after the 11 November engagement with the Italians.*

Below: *Bob Stanford-Tuck and some of his 257 Squadron pilots with souvenirs of the 11 November Regia Aeronautica raid.*

near Deal. Spitfires were scrambled and began to tussle with them, but two Jabos managed to get through to London, dropping their bombs on Charing Cross railway station. Five of the *Gruppe* failed to return, with a sixth crash-landing on the French coast. By this time other waves had been identified and Park had a number of squadrons in the air, the Spitfires sun up at 28,000 ft and the Hurricanes at 22,000 ft. For once his tactics worked perfectly. The Hurricanes were able to tackle the Jabos, while the Spitfires, with the advantages of sun and altitude tore into their escort, who quickly lost eleven. The Jabos jettisoned their bombs and retreated for home. Shortly afterwards the Me110s of *Eroberungsgrupe 210* made their last attack in the battle. Their target was the airfield at North Weald. They arrived just as the Hurricanes of 249 and 257 Squadrons were taking off, and managed to destroy two of them, as well as creating damage to the airfield and killing some twenty people on the ground. Their commander, now Otto Hintze, was, however, shot down and taken prisoner.

There was a bizarre end to the day, which marked the first daylight appearance of the *Regia Aeronautica*. Fifteen Savoia-Marchetti SM79 bombers, flying wing tip to wing tip, appeared over the Kent coast. They were accompanied by some 70 Fiat CR42 open cockpit biplane fighters. Faced with this strange spectacle, made even more peculiar by the exotic camouflage painting of the aircraft, it was some minutes before the ground defences opened fire. At that the Italians banked to the right and passed back over the coast of Ramsgate, dropping a few bombs on the town, and thence across the Channel once more. They would appear on just one more occasion, on 11 November, after the official end of the battle. Harwich was the target again, but the unfortunate Italians lost a total of 13 aircraft shot down.

30 October brought more rain and an unsuccessful attempt by the Jabos to get through to London. Luftwaffe losses were eight aircraft against five RAF. On the last day of the month there was no air activity by day and more rain. The Battle of Britain had ended.

MAUD

CHAPTER VII

THE AFTERMATH

American fighter pilots in the RAF. Some fought in the Battle and afterwards formed the famous Eagle squadrons.

Left: *Firewatchers during the London Blitz.*

Below left: *Aldwych Underground station plays host to refugees from the bombing.*

Right: *HM King George VI talking to Keith Park at Northolt, 26 September 1940.*

Below right: *The results of a Luftwaffe bomb on a London street.*

During the period 10 July – 31 October 1940 the Luftwaffe lost 1882 aircraft and RAF Fighter Command 1017. In human terms 537 British fighter pilots were killed and some 2600 German aircrew killed or captured. If casualties suffered by Bomber and Coastal Commands in their contribution to the battle are also taken into account, then the RAF suffered the loss of an additional 250 aircraft and 1000 aircrew. Viewed strictly in these statistical terms the Battle of Britain seems one of attrition, as indeed in many ways it was.

The Luftwaffe's aim was to achieve air supremacy over southern England in order to guarantee the success of SEALION. To do this it had to destroy RAF Fighter Command. Likewise, Dowding had to shoot down sufficient German aircraft to convince Goering that his continued efforts to achieve his objective were too costly to support.

The five phases of the battle reveal, however, that the Luftwaffe's analysis of its mission was found wanting in certain respects. The contact phase, which lasted up until 7 August, saw the Germans trying to tempt the RAF fighters into battle on advantageous terms to themselves. The bait was mainly attacks on Channel convoys, which meant that the Me109 could operate close to its airfields and hence its limited range was not a problem, while the British fighters could not afford to spend too long over the Channel. During this period Dowding's policy was one of conservation, especially trying to make good his losses suffered during the battle for France. Consequently he only tussled with the Luftwaffe when he had to do so.

The second phase, 8-23 August, was when the RAF came closest to defeat. It was not so much the destruction of its aircraft that so nearly brought this about, but the attacks on RAF Fighter Command's infrastructure. Dowding's approach to the air defence of Britain was a highly technical one. He saw his main force multiplier as the command, control, communications and intelligence (C^3I in modern parlance) system which he had so carefully constructed. The bedrock was the ability to get his fighters into the air in the right place and at the right time. If his C^3I system was so degraded that he was unable to do this then his numerical aircraft inferiority would become starkly revealed and he would be unable to close the floodgates. *Adlertag* and subsequent days saw heavy attacks on airfields and radar stations and stretched Fighter Command's infrastructure to breaking point. It was saved primarily by Goering's belief that attacks on the Chain Home network were not effective. As a result the Luftwaffe was drawn further towards London during the third phase, 24 August – 6 September, in its efforts to knock out more airfields and destroy Britain's fighter production. Yet, the further it was drawn inland the less effective the Me109, the primary weapon in the German armoury, became, because of its limited range.

The fourth phase, which lasted for the rest of September, saw London as the primary day target. This was part in reprisal for the RAF's raids on Berlin and part in the belief that the threat to the capital would draw more RAF fighters into the air to be shot down. There was, too, the idea of striking a blow at Britain's economy, an underlying theme from the onset of the battle, through bombing the London docks. Very quickly, though, the traditional airman's belief that attacks against civilian morale could be decisive emerged as the prime motive. The beginning of the Blitz by night demonstrated this only too clearly. Thus, while Hitler and Goering could kid themselves that five days of good weather would complete the task as far as SEALION was concerned, the truth was that Hitler had, in his own mind, gone off the idea of invasion by the

end of August. As early as 26 August he had ordered the first transfers of troops from France to Poland in preparation for the invasion of the Soviet Union, planning for which he had initiated in the middle of July. The events of 15 September in the skies above southern England merely reinforced his belief that the obstacle of the English Channel was too great. First he announced a postponement until spring 1941, and then on 12 October 1940 abandoned all invasion preparations. From then on it was little more than pride and frustration which caused the Luftwaffe to continue its attacks by day.

Yet, while the outcome of the battle was much influenced by German weaknesses and mistakes, it should not detract from the achievement of Dowding and his command. Dowding recognised above all the vital importance of keeping a reserve in being at all times. While he must have been tempted to commit many more squadrons than he did to the hard pressed 11 Group, he refused to be drawn and was proved right. He may have been a remote figure to his pilots and to have lived up to his nickname of 'Stuffy', but his calmness and singleness of purpose was well recognised by them. They were happy to refer to themselves, as Churchill called them at one point, as 'Dowding's chicks'.

Dowding's treatment after the battle was over has been the subject of much controversy ever since. It will be remembered that he was extended in command until October 1940. In the event, it was not until 24 November that he relinquished command, handing over to Sholto Douglas. In the meantime, on 30 September, in recognition of his efforts, he was made a Grand Commander of the order of the Bath (GCB). He was not, however, put on the retired list, but sent on a mission on behalf of the Ministry of Aircraft Production to the USA. He did not consider himself suited for this job, and it was not really a success since he had no business acumen. On his return he was asked to write his official dispatch on the Battle of Britain. He was then told that he was to be retired at the end of September 1941. But, then he was again asked to stay on in order to investigate ways in which economies could be effected in the RAF without loss of operational efficiency. By now he felt that he was not popular within the Air Ministry and his belief that this was so was reinforced when he discovered that his Dispatch had received only the most limited circulation within the Air Ministry. He did his best over the study, but most of his recommendations were not taken up and he considered this an indication that he had antagonised the Air Ministry even more. He retired finally in September 1942. Eventually, in May 1943, he was

Above: *601 Sqn Hurricane undergoing engine overhaul.*

Above left: *B D Russel who served in 1 (RCAF) Squadron during the Battle.*

Left: *41 Sqn Spitfire pilots wearing their Mae West lifejackets. Finlay, their CO, was a prewar Olympic hurdler.*

Right: *'Red' Tobin of 71 Eagle Squadron, who fought in 609 Squadron during the Battle. Note his arm insignia. His cry when scrambled was: 'Saddle her up, boys – I'm ridin'!'*

given a Barony. If he had been elevated to the peerage immediately after the battle and retired all might have been well. Unfortunately the continual changes of mind over retiring him and the two 'non jobs' that he was given after leaving Fighter Command preyed on his mind and convinced him that there was a conspiracy against him. The root of all these troubles was undoubtedly the clash between Leigh-Mallory and Park, and Leigh-Mallory's ill disguised low regard for Dowding. Leigh-Mallory considered that Park handled the battle in the wrong way in his piecemeal commitment of squadrons. This, however, showed a lack of understanding for Park's problems in the front line. As we have seen, the German tactics were designed to catch him wrong footed. He never knew when the next attack was coming and hence always had, just as Dowding did at the higher level, to keep something up his sleeve. He was constantly having to make knife edge decisions. No 12 Group, on the other hand, invariably had more warning of attacks and hence more time to concentrate their fighters than Park did. What also frustrated them so often, especially during the earlier phases, was they they were not called upon to assist No 11 Group as often as they felt they should have been. Their additional weight, they believed, would have resulted in many more German aircraft shot down. This was true, but what Leigh-Mallory did not recognise was that Park had to try and intercept the Luftwaffe attacks before they attacked his infrastructure, because if this was destroyed he was done for. Dowding recognised Park's problems, as did Brand, who experienced some of the same dilemmas. Yet, the fateful 17 October meeting left a sour taste in their mouths since it appeared to uphold, at least in the Air Ministry's eyes, that Leigh-Mallory was right and the others were wrong. On the surface of it, the subsequent careers of Park and Leigh-Mallory would appear to reinforce this.

Park was posted in December 1940 and sent to the seeming backwater of command of a training group. There was, however, no doubt that he was in need of a rest after the pressures of the past six months. He was succeeded in No 11 Group by Leigh-Mallory, who in 1941 took to the offensive, attacking the Luftwaffe across the Channel. In 1942 Leigh-Mallory succeeded Sholto Douglas as AOCinC Fighter Command and was elevated even higher in mid-1943 as AOCinC Second Tactical Air Force, the RAF component of the Allied Expeditionary Air Force (AEAF), and then the AEAF itself for the invasion of Europe. Park, on the other hand remained with No 23 Group until late 1941 when he was posted as Air Officer Commanding Egypt. In July 1942 he moved to Malta and conducted the defence of the island during the last phase of its long battle against the Axis air forces. He remained in the Mediterranean until the beginning of 1945, becoming supreme air commander in the Middle East in January 1944. In November 1944 Leigh-Mallory was appointed supreme air commander in South East Asia. However, he was killed in an air crash on the way out to Ceylon. His place was taken by Park. Thus, although Leigh-Mallory probably held the more glamorous posts, Park's subsequent career did not reflect any form of long-term slur.

The fates of the Luftwaffe commanders were also not affected by the fact that they had failed to win the battle. Goering remained as head of the Luftwaffe virtually to the end of the war and, after Rudolf Hess made his celebrated flight to Britain in May 1941, he became Deputy Führer. Kesselring was made Commander-in-Chief South in 1941 and was responsible for the higher direction of the German forces in North Africa. From autumn 1943 until the end of the war he conducted the Axis defence of Italy and in March 1945 also took over the crumbling Western Front. Sperrle remained in the West. He conducted the Blitz during winter 1940-41 and became Deputy Commander-in-Chief West. Stumpff, whose *Luftflotte 5* had such a brief and disastrous role in the battle, remained in Scandinavia until the end of 1943, when he took over *Luftflotte Reich*, responsible for the air defence of Germany itself.

As for the aircrews of both sides who took part in and survived the battle, some did not survive the war, falling in other air campaigns or being killed in air crashes. Among the latter was top ace Werner Mölders, by then Inspector of Fighter Aircraft, in November 1941. Others were captured, like Douglas Bader, who was shot down in a sweep over France in August 1941. Many, though, were still alive at the end of the war. Galland was a General, leading Me262s in combat against the Allies over Germany; Deere, and other leading RAF pilots in the battle, were commanding wings and groups.

Above: *122 Sqn Spitfires taking off from a satellite airfield. This squadron did not take part in the Battle and was formed in May 1941.*

Right: *Pilots of Canada's second fighter squadron, 402, which was formed in November 1940, race to their Hurricanes.*

The Blitz against London and other British cities continued throughout the winter and into the spring. It ended with a final massive attack on London on the night of 10/11 May 1941. After that the bulk of the Luftwaffe's strength was needed for Operation BARBAROSSA, the assault on Russia. British morale did not crack under this weight of bombing, thus seeming to show the prewar air prophets to be wrong, but how much longer they could have stood a prolonged bombing campaign cannot be judged. True, German morale endured a very much heavier and longer campaign, especially from 1943 onwards when the Americans joined Bomber Command in the strategic bombing offensive, but this debate is out of context in this book.

The Battle of Britain stands as a major turning point in the Second World War. It was the first German reverse of the war and brought Hitler to a halt in the West. It was not so much that the Luftwaffe was annihilated by the RAF; it was not. Rather, the Luftwaffe was prevented from achieving its objective. If it had, and by the end of August, SEALION would have taken place. If successful, Britain would have gone under. As to what might have happened then is for the reader to imagine. What is so is that it was the Royal Air Force's 'thin blue line' alone that stood between ultimate victory and total defeat in summer 1940. It was their 'finest hour'.

AE X
E S

INDEX

Page numbers in *italics* refer to illustrations

INDEX

Acknowledgments

The author and publishers would like to thank Mike Rose, who designed this book, and Ron Watson, who prepared the index. The following agencies and individuals supplied the illustrations on the pages noted.

AKG pages 39 below, 81 top
Archiv Gerstenberg pages 16-17 main picture, 32 below, 67 top
Mike Badrocke pages 38-39 artwork
Bildarchiv Preussischer Kulturbesitz pages 96-97 main picture
Bison Archive pages 7 below, 15, 16 both left, 17, 18 top, 20, 34 top, 35, 36, 37 both, 40, 41 both, 44 below, 46, 47 top, 56 left, 56-57 main picture, 58-59, 61 top, 64 top, 66-67, 70-71, 72-73, 81 centre and below, 82, 83, 84 both, 85 both, 89 below, 90 below, 101, 104 top, 108-109
Chaz Bowyer pages 1, 9 top, 22 below, 25 bottom two, 26-27 both, 30, 31 below, 39 top, 43, 47 below, 51 all 3, 53 top, 57, 58, 60, 65, 66 both, 67 bottom right, 68 below, 69 both, 70, 72 top, 73, 78 top, 79 top and centre, 90 top, 96 inset, 96-97 inset, 99 all three, 100, 105 top, 107 below /**IWM** page 50
Bundesarchiv pages 12, 13 both, 14-15, 28-29, 79 below
Norman Franks pages 4, 47 centre two, 48 both, 52 below, 53 below, 55, 80 both, 106 below /**IWM** page 52 top
John Frost Historical Newspapers page 86 below
Mike Hooks pages 34 below, 44 top
Robert Hunt Library pages 31 top, 64 below, 76 below, 78 below, 92-93
Imperial War Museum pages 2-3, 7 top, 8, 10-11, 14, 16 top right, 19 below, 21 both, 22 top, 23 both, 24 both, 32 top, 45, 54 below, 56 right, 61 below, 62-63, 68 top and centre, 72 below, 74-75, 76 top and centre, 86 top, 87 below, 88 below, 89 top, 91 both, 97, 98 top, 100-101, 104 below, 107 top
The Museum of London pages 77, 98 below
RAF Museum, Hendon page 87 top
Royal Canadian Air Force pages 9 below, 54 top, 59, 106 top, 109
TRH/BAe page 19 top,/**IWM** pages 102-103, /**RAF Museum** pages 6, 105 below, /**Vickers** page 18 below